STATISTICAL PACKAGE FOR THE SOCIAL

SPSS PRIMER

STATISTICAL PACKAGE FOR THE SOCIAL SCIENCES
PRIMER

**McGRAW-HILL
BOOK COMPANY**

New York
St. Louis
San Francisco
Auckland
Düsseldorf
Johannesburg
Kuala Lumpur
London
Mexico
Montreal
New Delhi
Panama
Paris
São Paulo
Singapore
Sydney
Tokyo
Toronto

WILLIAM R. KLECKA
Department of Political Science
and
Behavioral Sciences Laboratory
University of Cincinnati

NORMAN H. NIE
Department of Political Science
and
National Opinion Research Center
University of Chicago

C. HADLAI HULL
Computation Center
University of Chicago

Library of Congress Cataloging in Publication Data
Klecka, William R
    SPSS primer.
      1. SPSS (Electronic computer system) I. Nie,
Norman H., joint author. II. Hull, C. Hadlai,
joint author. III. Title.
H61.K55   300'.28'54   75-23306
ISBN 0-07-035023-X

SPSS PRIMER

7 8 9 0 WCWC 7 9

This book was set in Times Roman by Textbook Services, Inc.
The editors were Kenneth J. Bowman and Matthew Cahill;
the cover was designed by Joseph Gillians;
the production supervisor was Charles Hess.
Webcrafter, Inc., was printer and binder.

CONTENTS

8
DESCRIPTIVE STATISTICS AND ONE-WAY FREQUENCY DISTRIBUTIONS 60

9
CROSSTABULATIONS AND RELATED MEASURES OF ASSOCIATION: SUBPROGRAM CROSSTABS 70

10
SCATTER DIAGRAMS WITH BIVARIATE REGRESSION AND CORRELATION 82

As the use of the *Statistical Package for the Social Sciences* (SPSS) has grown, the demand for a short, introductory booklet has increased. This volume, the *SPSS Primer*, is a response to that need.

Our intention is not to provide a complete description of the SPSS language. Rather, our aim is to introduce the major features of SPSS at a simple, nontechnical level. Some technical material must be used, of course, but we have attempted to define important terms and to explain computer and statistical concepts as we go. We have even gone so far as to explain briefly the use and interpretation of the statistical techniques employed as examples in the latter chapters.

While writing the primer, we have kept two audiences in mind. One is the experienced researcher who wants to learn SPSS for use in work. Whether or not such an individual has had prior experience with computers, the primer should serve as an excellent self-study guide. The other audience is the student in any of a wide variety of courses in which the use of SPSS is being taught. Whether or not such courses deal exclusively with SPSS and whether they are methodological or substantive, we feel that this is an appropriate text for initiating the student into computerized statistical analysis.

Since it is an introduction, the primer cannot serve as a replacement for the SPSS manual, which documents the entire range of SPSS features. Thus, any of our readers who intend to make extensive use of SPSS, or who need features not covered here, are advised to continue their studies with the complete SPSS manual.

ACKNOWLEDGMENTS

As with most manuscripts, the cast of contributors goes well beyond the names on the cover. In this instance, credit should be given first to the many people who have made the SPSS programs possible. These include Karin Steinbrenner, the technical director of SPSS, and Jean G. Jenkins, programmer-analyst, who are in charge of the continuing development and maintenance of SPSS. ViAnn Beadle, the SPSS technical adviser, provides user consultation and testing, while Helena J. G. MacPherson, SPSS administrative assistant, and Patrick Bova of the National Opinion Research Center direct the distribution of the SPSS system. Jae-On Kim of the University of Iowa is the statistical consultant for SPSS. Dale H. Bent of the Faculty of Business Administration and Computing Services at the University of Alberta was one of the initial developers of SPSS along with Norman Nie and Hadlai Hull.

Most of the manuscript preparation was done at the University of Cincinnati. We wish to thank Linda Kocolowski for her valuable and insightful editorial suggestions and Alfred Tuchfarber for his technical review. The entire clerical staff at the Behavioral Sciences Laboratory typed the manuscript at one time or another, but the greatest burden was carried by Rachelle Boyle and Sandra Kraus. Our thanks also go to Eileen Petrohelos of the National Opinion Research Center, and to Kenneth J. Bowman, Matthew Cahill, and Charles Hess of McGraw-Hill for assistance in preparing this manuscript.

William R. Klecka
Norman H. Nie
C. Hadlai Hull

1
INTRODUCTION

Modern computers have dramatically increased the ease with which social scientists can analyze data. Today, most universities, larger businesses, and governmental agencies have some computing facilities. These machines can process large amounts of data and perform complex analyses with speed and efficiency. As a result, social scientists can study their data more thoroughly and can complete their research more quickly. This is true not only in academia, but in business and government also, where computers assist in studying many practical problems.

You as a researcher can gain access to the benefits of social science computing by learning one of the special languages used to communicate with the computer. One of the most popular and widely used languages for statistical analyses is SPSS which is short for *Statistical Package for the Social Sciences*. SPSS is a simple, consistent language which is easy to learn and does not require much knowledge about computers.

Virtually anyone who is willing to undergo a modest amount of training in SPSS can take advantage of contemporary methods of computerized data analysis. The fundamentals of that training are the subject of this primer. Before plunging into the details of the SPSS language, however, some background on the role of computers in social research is in order.

1.1 COMPUTERS AND SOCIAL RESEARCH

Computers contribute to social research in several ways. They are used for generating formal models of social systems, for simulating the behavior of nations or individual political actors, for organizing and retrieving large bodies of textual material such as abstracts of journal articles, and for analyzing the content of written works.

1

These complex electronic gadgets have made their most phenomenal impact, however, in the area of statistical computations.

In pre-computer days, researchers spent an inordinate amount of time in organizing their data and computing statistics by hand. Consequently, they tended to produce only the bare minimum number of tables required for the analysis. They also avoided the study of relationships involving several variables because of the immense amount of labor needed to produce the tabulations. Likewise, most researchers shunned complex and sophisticated statistical analyses, because the figures were difficult to compute on hand calculators and the likelihood of making errors was high. As a result, many important scientific questions went unanswered or were not pursued as well or as far as can be done today.

During the 1960s, computer technology advanced at a rapid pace. Not only did the machinery become faster and more versatile, but technicians developed easier means of communicating with computers. With minimal training and effort, the social researcher can now have the computer produce in a few seconds the tables and statistics that used to take hours, days, or weeks to prepare by hand.

The road to today's split-second statistics was not paved without difficulties, however. In the early days, only highly trained computer specialists were able to instruct the computer to perform a task. Such sets of instructions are called *programs,* and the specialists are called *programmers.* Social scientists and other researchers could not benefit greatly from the early computers unless they received sophisticated training in *programming*—the art of writing the special languages used in communicating with computers.

Recognizing this problem, programmers began developing generalized "packages" of programs for researchers to use in doing their own work. A *packaged program* is essentially a prepared program that will perform a specified set of operations, usually under the control of a simplified "language" or set of instructions. By mastering the simplified language, almost anyone can use the power of the computer without knowing much about how computers work.

SPSS is a packaged program specifically designed to compute those statistics typically used by social scientists. It was designed and developed during the late 1960s and is now one of the most widely used statistical packages.

Packaged statistical programs aid the research process beyond making data analysis quicker and easier. Normally, a researcher collects his data with certain expectations in mind about what his data will show. These expectations may be highly formalized theories and hypotheses or simply hunches and guesses about the nature of the real world. Either way, the researcher acquires a clearer picture of his subject matter after reviewing the first round of statistical analyses.

Typically the initial analysis, whether confirming or disproving the original expectations, raises new questions or suggests further avenues for study. This additional exploration is easily pursued because of the computer's speed and efficiency. The extra effort involved is so slight, in fact, that the researcher is encouraged to enter a repetitive sequence of analysis, reconsideration, further analysis, and further consideration. The end product is a deeper understanding of the subject matter well beyond the limits to which earlier researchers were able to go within a reasonable expenditure of time and effort.

1.2 PURPOSE OF THE SPSS PRIMER

Despite the great advances in computer technology, you will still have to learn a few things about how the machine works before you can use it to your advantage. Of course, instruction on the SPSS language is also needed. This is where the *SPSS Primer* comes in. The primer will introduce you to the fundamentals of computing with the *Statistical Package for the Social Sciences.* Because it is an introduction, the primer will focus strictly on the basic aspects of SPSS. The presentation will begin with background material on computers and then progress to information on how to: describe numerical data to SPSS; create and save a "system file" (an efficient way to store data, to be discussed later); recode data values; identify missing data; and use several of the more basic statistical procedures. Upon completing this text, you should be able to prepare a simple SPSS computer run for the analysis of your own data.

If you are planning to make extensive use of SPSS or if you need one of the features or statistical procedures not covered in the primer, you would do well to read the manual upon which this primer is based—*SPSS: Statistical Package for the Social Sciences,* by Norman H. Nie, C. Hadlai Hull, Jean G. Jenkins, Karin Steinbrenner, and Dale H. Bent (Second edition, McGraw-Hill Book Company, New York, 1975). Referred to here as simply "the SPSS manual," that larger book provides a complete description of the SPSS system. In particular, it describes alternate means of supplying data to SPSS, the use of alphabetic variables, the complete set of transformation instructions, the full range of statistical procedures, and numerous other details. In addition, the SPSS manual includes detailed descriptions of the statistics available in each of the statistical procedures, information which has been omitted from the primer because of space considerations.

2
AN INTRODUCTION TO COMPUTERS

Learning to use a computer is a lot like learning to drive a car. You do not need to know much about the internal workings to make good use of the machine. On a car you need to be able to find the ignition, steering wheel, and pedals. With computers you need a familiarity with computer cards, "files," and the control language necessary to tell the computer who you are and what you want. A very good automobile driver needs to know something about engines and transmissions in order to make the best use of his car, but he does not need to be an automotive engineer. Likewise, an intelligent social science computer user requires some acquaintance with the basic internal workings of the machine but not sophisticated training. This chapter will give you the computer basics you need to make you as comfortable using SPSS in your first computing endeavors as you were when driving your first car. If you are interested in learning more, you may consult some of the books listed at the end of this chapter.

2.1 PROGRAMS AND PROGRAM PACKAGES

A computer is only a machine—a mere automaton. While this fact may be obvious, it is worth emphasizing, for many people have the misconception that computers can "think." Despite the intriguing tales of science-fiction writers, computers can perform only the limited number of simple tasks built into their electronic circuitry. The machine executes these tasks only upon receiving specific instructions from some human user. By instructing the computer to execute the proper sequence of simple tasks, one can make it perform more complicated activities, such as calculating certain statistics for a given set of data. We refer to this series of instructions as a *program*.

A program is very much like a recipe. Consider the sequence of steps you go through if you are to bake a cake. First you read the recipe, and then you follow each

4

step in the order given. These steps include mixing the ingredients, pouring the mixture into a pan, and then placing it into a hot oven for a specified period of time. The *input* consists of the raw materials—in this instance, the flour, eggs, milk, and other ingredients. The *output* is the finished product—i.e., the cake. You, as the cook, transform the input into the output according to the instructions given in the recipe. In the process, you make use of an electric beater and an oven, which are specialized machines built to perform specific mechanical tasks under your control.

A computer functions in a similar manner. It must first read the program (the recipe) into its memory. Then it executes each program instruction until the end is reached. As an example, let us consider a program designed to compute the mean (the average) of a series of scores. The program would command the computer to read in the scores, add them up, and keep track of how many scores were read. When this is done, the computer would divide the sum by the number of scores to obtain the mean and would then write out the result. The input consists of the scores, while the mean constitutes the output. Of course, the computer needs a little help from its friends, the special devices for reading and writing.

While most programs are more complicated than this, they all work on the same general principle of a sequence of simple instructions. Figure 2.1 graphically illustrates the sequence of instructions needed to calculate the mean. After each step is completed, the next one is performed. At certain points, the computer must decide

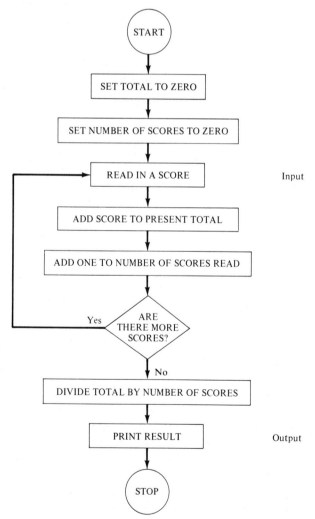

**FIGURE 2.1   Diagram showing sequence of steps taken to
compute the mean of a series of scores.**

whether to perform the next step or jump to some other specific point in the program. In our program, such a jump is necessary to repeatedly read single scores and process them until all scores have been read. Most statistical computations can, of course, be performed by humans using a desk calculator. In addition to the computer's phenomenal speed and accuracy, the computer's major advantage over a hand calculator is that the sequence of instructions can be built into a program which can be saved and used by anyone. Because statistical analyses are typically much more complicated than the computation of the mean, this is a great benefit, especially for researchers who are not mathematically inclined.

Specialized computers, such as those used to control guided missiles, have a single program built into their memory. We are concerned, however, with general-purpose computers. These differ from their specialized brothers and sisters by being able to accept and execute any number of programs. After the specified tasks of one program are completed, the general-purpose computer reads in another program and goes to work on it. Indeed, the more sophisticated computers can handle several programs simultaneously. This allows many people to make easy use of the same machine for a great variety of purposes.

Another important feature of general-purpose computers is that the programs prepared for them can be stored on some sort of recording medium, such as cards or magnetic tapes. In that form, the programs may be used repeatedly—with the same or different data—and may be transferred from one computer to another. This means that a researcher does not have to write a unique program each time he has a job for the computer. Indeed, he does not even have to know how to write programs if someone else has already prepared a program for the task he needs performed.

A *program package* is a series of prepared programs designed to perform related tasks. SPSS is an example. It is a compilation of many programs which compute those statistics typically needed by social science researchers. Program packages are of the greatest benefit in areas where many people need the same computer task (such as calculation of a certain statistic) performed under very similar conditions. Normally, the researcher needs to inform the package about which tasks he desires performed and something about the nature of his data. In SPSS, for instance, you can choose among many statistical procedures, and within each you can select specific processing modes and optional features. You also need to provide some details about your data, such as which variables to process and how many cases you have.

Users communicate with a program package through special instructions. In the more sophisticated packages, these instructions are given in the form of a simple written "language." By orienting the language to the subject matter of the programs, the package designers can create a system easily usable by persons unfamiliar with the inner operations of computers. Researchers can then take advantage of the computer's power merely by learning the special, simplified language for communicating with the package. This is the case with SPSS, and it is the purpose of this primer to train you in the fundamentals of the SPSS language.

2.2 COMPONENTS OF A COMPUTER

In our discussion of programs, we have implied that there are several distinct parts to the larger facility known as "the computer." This is quite true. Indeed, computers have three major functional areas: a central processing unit, a central memory, and a variety of input and output devices. The brief description of these components which follows will give you an idea of how the computer interacts with its human users and how it manages the many tasks assigned to it.

2.2.1 CENTRAL PROCESSING UNIT

The control and coordination of all activities are the responsibility of the *central processing unit* (CPU). This includes deciding which program to run next, bringing that program into central memory, executing the program instructions, and generally monitoring the machine's activities. In the larger and more sophisticated computers, the CPU can execute several programs simultaneously. To *execute* (or *run*) a program means to have the computer perform the instructions contained in the program.

When it is your program's turn to be executed, the CPU will read your job control instructions. *Job control instructions* are special instructions that allow you to communicate with the CPU. They serve mainly to inform the computer about which program is to be executed and what computer resources the program needs. These instructions are different in format and syntax from the SPSS language instructions. Since the "language" used for job control instructions is very different from one type of computer to another, it will not be discussed here. Suffice it to say that the job control instructions necessary to execute an SPSS program are usually simple and standardized. Most computing facilities have a handout and/or consultants available which will describe these instructions to you.

Mechanically, the CPU is composed of thousands of electronic components. Most of these are transistors and integrated circuits. The way in which these are put together and the kinds of components used greatly determine the speed and sophistication of the computer.

2.2.2 CENTRAL MEMORY

Central memory is used for storing program instructions and some data during the time that a program is actually operating. Sometimes referred to as "core storage," it is considered "central" memory because it is connected directly to the central processing unit (CPU). In contrast, external storage media, such as cards and tapes (to be discussed below), are used for long-term storage of information and can be considered another form of memory. External storage media can be detached, saved, and transported easily, while central memory cannot.

An important feature of central memory is that it is used to store information only temporarily. This information includes the program instructions, part of your data, and some results of the computations being performed. Once your program is finished, the computer reuses the central memory for the next program. Any of your information or results which were not written onto an external medium are then lost.

On computers capable of executing several programs simultaneously, you need to tell the computer how much of the central memory, or "core," is needed by your program. This varies from computer to computer, so you should check with your local computing facility for the details needed to run an SPSS program.

2.2.3 INPUT AND OUTPUT DEVICES

Modern computers use a variety of *input* and *output* devices. These serve as a means of communication between you and the machine. This communication takes place principally through the media of cards, printout paper, and/or remote terminals. Magnetic tapes and disks, however, are able to store large amounts of information, such as data and prepared programs, and can be used for both input and output. While tapes and disks can store information for very long time periods, they are also convenient for storing data temporarily, because they can be easily erased and reused. In the following sections, these typical input-output media will be explained and their utilization by SPSS users will be discussed.

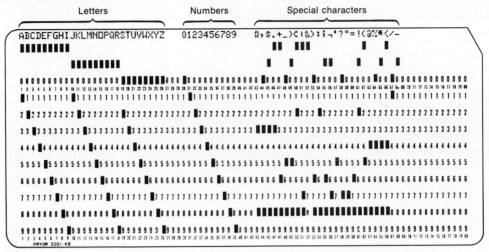

FIGURE 2.2   Example of a computer card punched with the IBM EBCDIC character set.

2.2.3.1 Computer Cards, the Card Reader, and the Punch

Most instructions and data are given to SPSS on *computer cards*. These oblong pieces of stiff paper come in a variety of colors and printed designs. The color and printing on the card make no difference to the computer, however, because the machine reads only the holes that have been punched into the card. An example of a typical computer card is given in Fig. 2.2.

Each card has room for 80 characters of information. Each *column* is a vertical position capable of holding a single character. *Characters* are single digits, letters, and other symbols represented by one or more holes punched in the same column. Every column has 12 positions (corresponding to "rows" on the card) in which a hole may be punched. The bottom 10 are numbered from zero through nine. A single punch in a column falling in one of these positions is interpreted as the corresponding number. The top two rows are often referred to as the "12" and "11" positions, although as single punches they represent specific characters, such as the ampersand and dash. The other characters are created by various combinations of two or three punches in the same column, as can be seen in Fig. 2.2.[1] A blank column (no holes) is also considered a character.

The machine you use for punching information onto cards is called a *keypunch*. The keypunch is similar to an electric typewriter. The main difference is that holes are punched into cards instead of letters being typed onto paper. Blank cards (that is, cards without any holes) are placed in a hopper on the right-hand side of the keypunch. Under your control, the keypunch feeds the cards, one at a time, into the punching mechanism. As you hit the keys on the keyboard, the holes corresponding to that character are punched into the column that is under the punching mechanism. Finished cards are stacked on the left-hand side. The keyboard is very similar to that of a typewriter. Numbers and some special characters are in different locations, however, and there are no lowercase letters. The keypunch is easy to use even if you do not know how to type. Your computing facility personnel can teach you how to operate one.

Cards are read by the computer through a machine called a *card reader*. The card reader "reads" cards by electronically sensing the holes in each column and translating them into appropriate electronic impulses.

---

[1]There are two major systems for representing characters by hole combinations. The older method is called BCD (Binary Coded Decimal), while the newer system, which is used by almost all IBM computers, is called EBCDIC (Extended Binary Coded Decimal Interchange Code). EBCDIC has 14 additional characters, and some of the special characters have different hole combinations. These systems are not completely standardized, because each computer manufacturer has its own special version. As an SPSS user, however, you normally need not concern yourself with these nuances.

SPSS and some other computer programs occasionally produce information intended to be punched out onto cards. This information may be a correlation matrix, a new version of your data, or other information that is likely to be read into the computer at a future time. The *card punch* is the machine which punches the information sent directly from the computer.

2.2.3.2 High-Speed Line Printer

Usually part or all of the results produced by a program are returned in printed form. This printing is done by a machine called a *line printer* or, more simply, *the printer*. Electronic impulses from the computer are converted into the appropriate characters as the printer produces each line. SPSS, of course, produces printed output consisting mostly of the tables and statistics you have requested.

2.2.3.3 Magnetic Tapes

Magnetic tapes are an external storage medium resembling the tapes used in tape recorders. Computer tapes are thin plastic strips coated on one side with a magnetic recording substance. Reading and writing are done by the computer through a machine called a *tape drive*. As with a regular tape recorder, the tape drive can sense the magnetic information and can put new information onto the tape by changing the magnetic fields. Because information is stored very compactly on tapes, a 2,400-foot reel can hold as much data as hundreds of thousands of cards. SPSS users often use tapes for the long-term storage of their data and to facilitate the transportation of their data from one computing facility to another. Tapes are especially useful when more than a few hundred cards are needed to hold your data.

A very useful feature of magnetic tapes is that they can hold many sets of information referred to as "files." A *file* is a distinct group of information separated from another group by a tape mark (a special magnetic code). To better understand the concept of a file, think of a reel of tape as being somewhat like an office filing drawer. The filing drawer contains many folders, each called a file. Within these files are several papers, often referred to as "records." A magnetic tape can likewise be subdivided into tape files with each file containing a series of magnetic records. A *magnetic record* is a series of contiguous, magnetically stored items of information. Records are written in a series, one after the other, on the tape. They are separated from each other by a short portion of blank tape. These magnetic records often correspond to computer cards, although they are not necessarily restricted to holding only 80 columns of information. Each tape file contains a different set of data or other information. Several files may be stored together on a tape for the sake of convenience and to utilize empty space.

2.2.3.4 Disk Packs and Similar Devices

Another commonly used input/output device is the disk pack. A *disk pack* is an external storage medium composed of several platters coated with a magnetic film. Each platter (more properly referred to as a "disk") resembles a large phonograph record. Several are stacked together on a vertical spindle, but they are positioned one inch apart. Information is stored on a disk pack in the form of records and files somewhat similar to those found on magnetic tape. The machine which transfers information back and forth between the disk pack and the computer is called a *disk drive*.

Disk packs are especially useful for storing packaged programs, such as SPSS, and data sets which are used very frequently. They are also a convenient medium for temporarily storing data and other information while they are in use by a program. As you will learn later, SPSS produces a "system file" during the process of analyzing your data. Normally, this file is most efficiently kept on a disk pack during the time SPSS is actually processing it.

Other input/output devices also exist, including drums and data cells. Each has its special advantages and applications. Because they are not employed as commonly as tapes and disk packs and because you are not likely to need them in your use of SPSS, they will not be discussed here.

2.2.3.5 Remote Terminals

While cards and printout are good media for communicating with the computer, they necessitate using the computer in batch mode. *Batch mode* is a procedure for handling computer jobs where your job is read in with a batch of others and waits its turn before executing. Depending upon how busy the computer is, the time between reading in and receiving the printed output, known as *turnaround time,* can be anywhere from a few minutes to many hours.

Interactive mode is an alternative method for utilizing the computer in which instructions are acted upon immediately. This is achieved through the use of *remote terminals* which resemble electric typewriters. They are connected with the computer either directly by a cable or indirectly through telephones. Actually, there are several different styles of remote terminals. Some are specially adapted electric typewriters, others are the standard teletype machine, while others have a video screen (like a television tube) connected to a keyboard.

The basic principle of interactive mode is that commands are typed in via the terminal and acted upon immediately. How this works depends upon the control program to which the terminal is connected. Sometimes, computational tasks, such as computing correlation coefficients from a given set of data, are actually performed while you wait. This is pure interactive computing. Other interactive arrangements, however, allow you to create only files of instructions and data, which can then be "submitted" as though they were cards. Jobs submitted in this fashion are executed in batch mode, with the printed results being sent either to the line printer or your terminal. Interactive computing methods allow use of the computer from any place having a telephone, and they usually include other features which make computer usage easier.[1]

Another type of remote "terminal" which is worth mentioning is the *remote job entry station*. This is merely a card reader, printer, and possibly other equipment connected to a distant computer via cable or telephone. Except for its physical separation from the main computer, it acts like a normal card reader and printer, allowing only batch jobs.

2.3 HOW COMPUTERS HANDLE NUMBERS

Computers handle numbers and data in several forms: as characters, integer numbers, and floating-point numbers. A basic understanding of how these differ is important to you, because SPSS does not make full use of all three modes.

With *character storage mode,* also called "alphanumeric," any allowable character (letter, digit, or other symbol) is stored in a single location according to a given electronic pattern. This type of storage is similar to the way characters are stored on a card. The important thing is that numerical digits stored in character mode do not have an electronic pattern appropriate for meaningful arithmetic computations. While the computer can go through the motions of arithmetic when handling character mode data, the results are meaningless. SPSS is unusual in allowing users to supply character mode data. Usage of character data in SPSS is very limited, however. For most statistical procedures, such data must be transformed into numerical values before they are used. (See the SPSS manual for details on handling character data.)

With *integer storage mode* numbers are stored as electronic impulses represent-

---

[1]The version of SPSS to be described in this primer was designed for card input, although it can be used with the latter type of terminal system where batch jobs are created interactively. A truly interactive version of SPSS is under development but has not been completed at the time of this writing.

ing merely integers (whole numbers) without fractional parts. Since almost all statistical routines either allow fractional numbers as data or compute decimal fractions as answers, integer mode is impractical for statistical programs. Thus, SPSS does not allow you to store your data internally in integer mode.

Floating-point storage mode (also referred to as "real" numbers) is used for storing numbers with decimal fractions. (The term "floating point" comes from the fact that the computer converts these numbers into a form resembling "scientific notation." This is where the decimal point is moved to a position in front of the first nonzero number, and the result must then be multiplied by the number 10 raised to the appropriate power.) This type of numeric representation allows the use of the full range of arithmetic computations. Numbers that are actually integers may be stored in floating-point mode, too. They are treated, however, as having a zero fractional portion (i.e., the integer 2 would be interpreted as 2.000, etc.). Indeed, it is usually possible to omit the decimal point (even for fractions) when keypunching data (see Sec. 5.2.3 in the primer and the discussion of input formats in the larger manual).

The three storage modes just presented are the forms in which the computer stores and manipulates data *internally*. The data you punch onto cards, however, are actually an external character form—even the numerical digits. When any program reads data cards, it must convert the external form into one of the three internal forms just described. Programmers often refer to the internal representation of data as *binary mode,* regardless of the type. (This is because the electronic patterns used to represent the data inside the machine are based upon an adaptation of the binary numbering system.) Although data are never punched in binary form, SPSS and other programs will sometimes write data in binary form onto tapes and disks for the sake of efficiency.

REFERENCES

BOLT, A. B., and M. E. WARDLE: *Communicating with a Computer.* New York: Cambridge University Press, 1970.

HARKINS, PETER B., THOMAS L. ISENHOUR, and PETER C. JURS: *Introduction to Computer Programming for the Social Sciences.* Boston: Allyn and Bacon, 1973.

JANDA, KENNETH: *Data Processing,* 2d ed. Evanston: Northwestern University Press, 1969.

KATZAN, HARRY JR.: *Computer Organization and the System/370.* New York: Van Nostrand Reinhold Company, 1971.

MCCRACKEN, D. D.: *A Guide to FORTRAN IV Programming.* New York: John Wiley & Sons, Inc., 1965.

RALSTON, ANTHONY: *Introduction to Programming and Computer Science.* New York: McGraw-Hill Book Company, 1971.

3
PREPARING DATA FOR STATISTICAL ANALYSIS

Before plunging into the specifics of the SPSS language, we need to cover some basic points about social science data. The concepts of a data case and a variable need to be clarified, and you need some information about the form in which SPSS expects to receive the data. Let us begin, though, with a brief discussion of where social science data come from.

3.1 WHERE DATA COME FROM

The diversity of human activities provides a myriad of subjects for study. The scientific investigation of these activities, however, normally requires the collection of empirical data in a systematic fashion. *Empirical data* are facts recorded through observation of events or characteristics. The observation may be a very simple act, such as counting the children in a family, or a very complex activity, like determining the gross national product of a nation. Either way, some sort of sensory perception is necessary.

The data that you as a social scientist use in your research may come from a variety of sources. You may collect them yourself by personally asking people questions or observing their activities. Sometimes the assistance of a staff or a research organization is necessary. An organization or project director needing survey data, for example, might hire a survey research firm to conduct the interviews. Often social data are collected and distributed by a public or private agency. Voting returns, census statistics, and corporate financial reports are just a few examples. Data archives are another important source of data. Most major universities have some sort of social science data archiving facility which stores data much as a library stores books. Archived data, often recorded on computer cards or tapes, are usually collected for a specific project and then saved because of their potential use to future researchers.

An important distinction to keep in mind is the difference between "data" and a "statistical program." Some beginning computer users have the mistaken notion that the data come with the program. A statistical program will process any data given to it in the proper form. The data are completely separate, however, and must be acquired and prepared by the user. Often researchers or the staff of a data archive will store data in the form of an SPSS system file. This makes the data easier to use in future analyses, but the data file itself is separate from the program and unavailable to it until you instruct the computer to access that file. In particular, SPSS has nothing to do with collecting or creating the data.

3.2 CASES, VARIABLES, AND THE ACT OF MEASUREMENT

When using SPSS, as in most social science research, the *case* is the basic unit of analysis. A case might be an individual respondent in a sample survey, a subject in an experiment, or some larger entity such as a city, nation, or institution. Occasionally, a case is a more abstract unit such as an experimental condition or a time interval. Very basically, cases are the things on which measurements are taken.

When collecting data, we usually measure several variables at a time. A *variable* is an observable entity which can take on more than one value or characteristic. A family's life style, a person's opinion of the President, and the population of a city are all variables (assuming we are studying more than one family, person, or city or that we are studying them at different points in time). On the other hand, the length of a yardstick and the number of home runs hit by Babe Ruth are not variables, because they are fixed quantities. The variables measured during a study then become the objects of our statistical analysis.

The act of recording an observation is known as *measurement*. Proper measurement entails assigning a value or score to the observed phenomenon. A *value* is simply a coded symbol to represent the status of the observed phenomenon. Some variables have obvious numeric values which can be used for the measurement, such as a city's population or a student's exam score. Other variables require an arbitrary coding scheme to identify the various conditions. An example of this type would be assigning the number 1 to a male respondent and the number 2 to a female respondent. The assigned value, then, corresponds to the result of our observation. When we intend to analyze the data with the aid of a computer, we normally employ only numeric values, because these are easier for the computer to manipulate.

The rules which define the assignment of an appropriate value determine the *level of measurement*. The different levels are defined on the basis of the ordering and distance properties inherent in the measuring rules. You need to know these rules and their implications, because each statistical technique is appropriate for data measured only at certain levels. For instance, crosstabulations can be performed for any level of measurement, but regression analysis requires data measured at what we call the interval or ratio levels. Unfortunately, the computer does not know what level of measurement underlies the numbers it receives. Thus, it is up to you to determine whether a particular technique is suitable for your data.

A complete discussion of levels of measurement is given in the SPSS manual and most introductory social science texts. But because later chapters of the primer make occasional references to the various levels, a brief summary follows.

Any valid measurement scheme requires that each possible observation can be assigned to one and only one distinct value. If the values used serve merely as labels or names for the category, then the measurement is at the *nominal level*. Here, we make no assumption about ordering or distances between categories. For instance, a person's religion is a nominal variable.

When all of the categories can be ranked according to some criterion of order, we have the *ordinal level* of measurement. For example, the classification of social classes as working, middle, and upper is ordered according to status.

In addition to a criterion of ordering, the *interval level* of measurement includes a definition of the distances between the categories in terms of fixed and equal units. A thermometer records temperatures in terms of degrees, and a 1° increase in the temperature implies the same amount of additional heat whether the change is at the lower end of the scale or at the upper.

The *ratio level* of measurement has all of the properties of an interval scale with the addition that a zero point is inherently defined by the measurement scheme. Thus, when we measure physical distances, a zero distance is naturally defined: it is the absence of any distance between two objects. On the other hand, the Fahrenheit and Centigrade systems for denoting temperature do *not* qualify as ratio measures because their zero points are arbitrary.

Because the meanings of the numeric codes used for variables are not always apparent, you should thoroughly document your coding schemes. A *codebook* is the document that describes each variable. This includes the variable's meaning, the codes used and their meanings, where the variable is punched on the data cards, and the brief name used to reference the variable in SPSS (see Sec. 4.1.2.1 for an explanation of "variable names").

Examples of two codebooks are in Appendix A. These codebooks describe the variables from two studies to be used as examples throughout the primer. The first of these is the "American Small Communities Study," which contains several types of data on 64 small towns and cities. For the sake of brevity, we will refer to this data set as the COMSTUDY file. The other set of data is derived from a survey of individuals concerning membership and activity in various clubs. We have named this data set the ORGSTUDY file. In both studies, only one data card is needed for each case.

As you can see, these codebooks have been divided into three vertical sections. The leftmost section contains the column numbers in which each variable has been punched on the data cards, and the second section reports the SPSS variable name. (The assignment of these two pieces of information and their use in creating the SPSS system file will be discussed in a later section of this chapter and in subsequent chapters.) The right-hand portion contains the detailed description of each variable, including an explanation of the coded values.

For most of the variables in the COMSTUDY file, exact values of the variable as measured constitute the data. This means that the variable POP60, for instance, contains the exact population for the community as of 1960. The first community listed had a population of 8,350, so the number "8350" was punched in columns 34 through 37 of the first data card. No special coding scheme was used to report the population. In contrast, the variable HRSWORK has the number of hours worked by the head of government divided into six groups plus two additional categories for situations which did not apply or where data were not available. If the government head for some city reported working 25 hours per week, the code value " 4" was punched in column 68 of that city's data card.

Quite often in social science research, a valid measurement cannot be made on a variable for some of the cases. When this happens, you have *missing data*. In survey research, this frequently occurs because respondents answer with "Don't know" or refuse to answer certain questions. When studying cities, nations, or institutions, certain pieces of information may not be available for every unit. This presents special problems for the data analyst. Some sort of value should be assigned for those cases as they are punched onto the computer cards. Yet, that value will not normally fit into the legitimate measurement scheme, and you will usually want to omit those cases from analyses employing that variable. SPSS helps you to solve this problem by permitting up to three different missing value codes for each variable. (Sec. 5.5 explains how you communicate this to SPSS.) When SPSS comes across these cases while analyzing that variable, the cases are omitted from that tabulation (unless you specially request that they be retained). In the codebooks given in Appendix A, the symbol (MV) follows the categories declared as missing values when the data were made into an SPSS system file.

3.3 PREPARING DATA CASES FOR SPSS INPUT

Generally, variables are punched onto computer cards in a fixed-column format so that each case occupies one or more cards. In *fixed-column format*, the values of each variable are located in the same columns for every case. When a case is made up of more than one card, the variable must be entered on the same card for each case. For example, if John Doe's age is punched in columns 6 and 7 on the third card of his case, the age of every other respondent in the study would also occupy columns 6 and 7 of the third card of their cases.

Figure 3.1 shows three examples of cases organized in fixed-column format. In the first example, there is one card per case; in the second example there are two cards per case; and in the third example, there are four cards per case. A case may continue from one physical card to another, and there is no fixed limit to the number of cards a case may contain. However, no variable *value* may be continued from one card of a case to another; each value must be wholly contained on a single card, because of the system used by the computer to translate punches into the internal representation of numbers. The cards constituting each of the cases must be in the same sequence (because the variable order in each case must be the same), but the cases themselves need not be sequenced. Blank spaces need not be included between each variable as was done in Fig. 3.1(a). Although blank spaces may make it easier for you to read the card, the computer does not need them, and the extra space and effort required to enter them may not be justified.

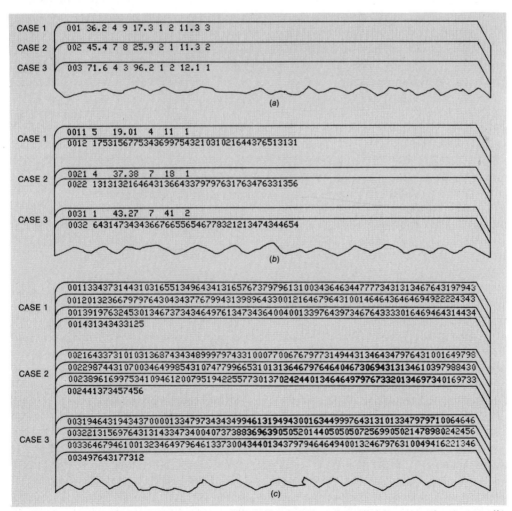

FIGURE 3.1   Examples of data cards punched in fixed-column format. (a) one card per case; (b) two cards per case; (c) four cards per case.

Identification numbers may also be punched on the data cards. A unique case-identification number should be assigned to each case and punched on every card associated with that case. If there are more than one card per case, a card-sequence number should also be assigned (i.e., 1 for the first card in each case, 2 for the second, etc). Regardless of whether or not you have SPSS process these case and card numbers, these identification variables may be helpful to you. Among other uses, they allow you to reorder your data cards in the event they are dropped or otherwise disarranged. Identification numbers also permit you to refer back to the original data source to clear up doubts about the accuracy of the punched cards. Further, you may manipulate these identification numbers as any other variable when processing the data. Even if you supply your own identification numbers, SPSS itself assigns a unique sequence number to each case as it is read. This sequence number is automatically present whenever the file is processed. (See the SPSS manual for further details.)

Once the data have been coded and punched, they may be read into SPSS directly from punched cards. Alternately, they may be copied onto a tape or disk file and read into SPSS at a later time. The SPSS system can read data from any machine-readable device or medium which can be used with your local computer. Futhermore, the data need not be in card-image records (i.e., they may be stored as records which are longer or shorter than 80 columns).

There is no programmed limit to the number of cases which can be entered into an SPSS file. In practice, however, the upper limit is to some degree fixed by the amount of direct-access (i.e., disk, data cell, and/or drum) storage available for temporary use at your computer installation. If you have a very large number of cases, you may want to check with your local computing facility consultants about the adequacy of direct-access storage.

Irrespective of the number of cases in a file, you may not enter more than 500 variables into a single SPSS file. This limit applies to the regular version of SPSS. Note, however, that you may create and use a special "archive file" with up to 5,000 variables by using special features decribed in the SPSS manual. A special version of SPSS, called SPSS-maxi, exists. With SPSS-maxi you may read-in and process up to 1,000 variables at a time. Of more interest to you as a beginner, however, is another special version called SPSS-mini. SPSS-mini has the capacity of handling only up to 100 variables at a time. Also, it usually produces fewer tables per statistical request. The great advantage of SPSS-mini is that it requires less core storage while executing. This makes it particularly useful for training purposes and smaller research problems.

Your variables may take on almost any numeric value. The computer, however, will accurately store only the first six significant digits. Also, SPSS does not display extremely large or extremely small (fractional) values very well when it prints your results.

3.4 SPSS SYSTEM FILES

One of the special advantages of SPSS is that it converts your data into a *self-describing system file*. This is a special file containing all the information SPSS needs to identify your variables (i.e., variable names, labels, missing value codes, etc.) plus the data themselves. These are all stored in binary mode on a tape or disk in the most efficient form for future use. With a system file you can repeatedly access your data with ease. Variable locations and labels need be provided only once, the chance of accessing the wrong information is reduced, and less computer time is needed.

The system file is actually created in two steps. During your initial SPSS run, it is necessary to provide SPSS with a series of instructions that describe your data. This is called *defining the file,* and the procedure is explained in Chap. 5. The labels you provide, if any, and a few other pieces of documentary information are written onto a temporary label file. When the statistical procedures need labels for the printed output, they are retrieved from this file. During the execution of your first statistical procedure, SPSS reads the data, converts them to the appropriate internal representation (binary), makes a copy of the binary data on a temporary tape or disk file, and provides to the statistical procedure the variables it needs. The temporary data file is then used by all the subsequent statistical procedures as the most efficient means of reaccessing the data.

The operations just described are always performed whenever you give the original raw data to SPSS. These temporary files, however, are lost by the computer at the end of your run, unless you take special actions to save them. A system file is saved by giving SPSS a SAVE FILE command (to be explained in Sec. 5.9.1). SPSS will then copy both the label and the data files onto a single permanent file. You can use this permanent system file in future SPSS runs for easy access to the data without the need to redescribe each variable.

4
SPSS CONTROL CARDS

Up to this point you have been learning about computers and data preparation. This has been important background information which will make your use of SPSS easier and more efficient. Now it is time to begin learning the language by which you can communicate with SPSS. This language is "spoken" through the medium of *control cards*, each being a specific command similar to a sentence. In this chapter, you will learn the basic building blocks of the SPSS language and the general rules for combining these into meaningful commands. In subsequent chapters you will learn the specific rules that apply to the individual control cards being described in the primer. As you will see, SPSS is much easier to learn than a natural language, because it is limited to one specific topic.

4.1 CONTROL-CARD PREPARATION: GENERAL SYNTAX RULES

Control cards perform many functions in the SPSS system. Some of the cards define and describe the data that are to be entered into the system; others allow you to control the operation of the statistical procedure being used; yet others enable you to modify the data in your file.

Although each control card in the SPSS system has a unique function, all the cards share a common format, and information is entered onto them in a similar manner. The control-card language is a very simplified quasi-natural language consisting of names, values, keywords, and rules governing punctuation and spacing.

All SPSS control cards have two parts, or fields. A *field* is merely a group of contiguous columns. The *control field* occupies card columns 1 through 15 and contains the *control word or words* which identify the card to you and the system. The *specification field* occupies card columns 16 through 80 of that and all subsequent cards necessary to complete the specifications. In the specification field, you will enter the information required by the particular control card being used.

4.1.1 CONTROL FIELD

Each control card is identified by a unique control word or set of control words. These control words tell SPSS the type of action to be performed and the kind of specifications required so that SPSS can read, interpret, and act upon the information on that card.

The control field is always punched in card columns 1 through 15 and always begins in column 1. The control words that occupy this field are of various lengths, but they never exceed 15 characters. The spelling and spacing of control words must conform exactly to the samples presented in the primer. The following are a few examples of control fields which are used in the SPSS system:

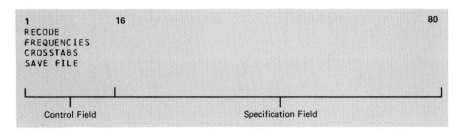

```
1               16                                                      80
RECODE
FREQUENCIES
CROSSTABS
SAVE FILE
```

Control Field   Specification Field

The meanings of these example control cards will be explained fully in subsequent chapters. Very briefly, though, these control cards initiate the following operations: (1) change the coding scheme on one or more variables; (2) compute and print one-way frequency counts on the variables specified; (3) compute and print one or more crosstabulations as specified; and (4) save the data in a system file.

4.1.2 SPECIFICATION FIELD

In the field occupying card columns 16 through 80, you supply the system with the detailed instructions required to perform the task needed in your specific situation. (A few control cards require no specifications, in which cases the specification fields are left blank.) The specifications may be the name of a file, variable names, labels, instructions about the desired tables, or one of many other types of information. The following are some examples:

```
1               16
FILE NAME       EXAMPLE, EXAMPLE OF FILE NAME AND LABEL
CROSSTABS       TABLES = SEX BY RACE
```

As you will learn later, the first command assigns the name EXAMPLE and the associated label to the SPSS system file. The second command asks for a crosstabular table of the variable SEX by the variable RACE.

Specification fields are like sentences, because they are composed of words and punctuation arranged in a meaningful fashion. In SPSS, there are six types of words and punctuation, which we refer to as *elements*. The six types are *names, values, keywords, labels, delimiters,* and *operators*. The elements which make up a specification must be placed in card columns 16 through 80, never in card columns 1 through 15. The specifications may continue from one physical card to the next as long as columns 1 through 15 of all subsequent cards used to complete the specification are left blank. Examples of the flexibility of locating elements on the cards and the use of continuation cards are given in later parts of this chapter and throughout the primer.

4.1.2.1 Names

Names are used for referring to variables and files. Just as any proper name allows us to easily refer to specific people, places, and things, SPSS names enable us to tell SPSS which variables and files to use and analyze. For example, SEX and AGE are obvious names for variables which are almost always included in studies of individual people. Names should be as clearly descriptive as possible. Unfortunately, some things are not as easily named as sex and age; but the more descriptive the names are, the easier it will be for you to keep track of variables and files.

Names may be from one to eight characters in length, and the first character must be an *alphabetic letter*. Otherwise, names may be composed of letters and/or numbers, but special characters may not be used. *Special characters* are defined as all characters which are not letters or numbers. This includes all punctuation marks. Names must be single words; that is, they may not contain imbedded blanks. Several examples are given below, along with typical errors in creating names:

(Correct)	(Incorrect)
NETWORTH	NET WORTH
JOB2	2NDJOB
EDUC	EDUCATION
SEXROLE	SEX-ROLE

NET WORTH is incorrect because it contains an internal blank. SPSS would interpret this as two distinct names, which was not the intention. 2NDJOB erroneously begins with a number, EDUCATION is too long, and SEX-ROLE contains a special character (i.e., a hyphen).

Furthermore, when you are writing a name in an SPSS instruction, you must keep the entire name on a single card. You can continue the specification field onto the next card, but not a name.

4.1.2.2 Values

A *value* is any fixed numeric quantity or score or an alphabetic code. The values most commonly used in SPSS instructions are specific values of your variables. For instance, on a MISSING VALUES card you specify the values corresponding to missing data codes. There are also several other places where values are entered—for example, when you indicate the number of cases in the file or specify desired statistics and options. These uses will be explained in later chapters.

Values, like all other pieces of information in the specification field, must be composed of contiguous characters; i.e., they may not contain blanks. Individual values, just as with names, must be contained on a single punched card. If the card you are punching does not have enough room left for the next value, name, or whatever, leave that space blank and continue on the next card. Extra blanks *between* the elements of an SPSS instruction are quite acceptable, though.

Numeric values may be either integers or decimal numbers. Zeros in the left-hand portion of *numeric* values may be deleted even though the values on the data cards may have such leading zeros. Thus, the values 01, 098.6, and 0.432 and the values 1, 98.6, and .432 are equivalent. Alphabetic values are handled in a special fashion not described in this primer, but they are covered in the SPSS manual.

4.1.2.3 Keywords

Keywords are specially defined words which have a particular meaning in the SPSS system. Some examples of keywords are TO, THRU, BY, and WITH. Each of these has a specific use, which will be described in later chapters. As a general rule, however, keywords must be punched exactly as described, and, like names and values, individual keywords must not contain imbedded blanks or be split between two cards.

4.1.2.4 Labels

The SPSS system has a large number of labeling features. Files, variables, and variable values may be given extended labels which appear automatically on printed output. *Labels* are optional, extended, documentary information. An entire label is considered a single element and is printed just as it is entered on the control card. An example of one type of label was given at the beginning of Sec. 4.1.2, where the FILE NAME command was illustrated. In that example, the file name EXAMPLE was followed by the label "EXAMPLE OF FILE NAME AND LABEL." Unlike any of the other elements of an SPSS instruction, individual labels may be continued from one punched card to the next if necessary. Several different types of labels exist, and each is described fully in Chap. 5.

4.1.2.5 Delimiters

Individual names, values, keywords, and labels appearing in the specification field must be separated from one another by delimiters. *Delimiters* are certain characters used to separate the various parts of an instruction. They are the punctuation of the SPSS language. Two different types of delimiters are used in SPSS—common and special.

The blank and the comma are the *common delimiters*. They are always used to separate elements unless one of the special delimiters is required. The blank and the comma are equivalent and may be used interchangeably, depending upon your preference.

Additional blanks and/or commas may be inserted between elements to improve readability, as illustrated in the following examples:

```
1               16
FREQUENCIES     GENERAL = AGE SEX RACE
FREQUENCIES     GENERAL = AGE,SEX,RACE
FREQUENCIES     GENERAL=AGE, SEX,    RACE
FREQUENCIES     GENERAL = AGE
                SEX
                    RACE
```

The above four commands are all correct and equivalent means of requesting frequency counts on the variables AGE, SEX, and RACE (see Chap. 8 for details). In the first command, each element is separated by a single blank. In the second example, only commas separate the variable names. For the third, there are no common delimiters around the equals sign, because they are not actually required there, as you will learn in a moment. In addition, the variable names are separated by commas *and* one or more blanks. The last example illustrates the continuation of a command onto subsequent cards. Columns 1 through 15 are left blank on the continuation cards and the continuation begins in either column 16 or any later column. This also illustrates that many blanks may separate the elements and that you do not need to fill one card before beginning a continuation card. Unless a special delimiter is present, you need at least one common delimiter, but whether you use blanks, commas, or both and how many depend upon your preferences.

There are four *special delimiters*: the *left parenthesis* [(], the *right parenthesis* [)], the *equals sign* [=], and the *slash* [/]. The left and right parentheses are always used in conjunction with each other, and their most common usage is that of setting off a list of values. The equals sign is used to separate a keyword from values or special instructions. The slash is often used to separate certain portions of a single command. It can also mean that one set of specifications has been completely entered and that you are about to begin a new and independent set of specifications.

The four special delimiters are employed only when the specific format of a control card calls for their use. The MISSING VALUES card, for example, requires that the missing values be enclosed in parentheses and that the missing values which apply to one variable be set off from the next variable name by a slash. A sample MISSING VALUES card might appear as follows:

```
1          16
MISSING VALUES INCOME (0,8,9)/RACE (3)
```

Detailed rules for the MISSING VALUES and other control cards are given in later chapters.

Common delimiters (blanks and/or commas) are not required to further separate special delimiters from each other or from other elements. But you can insert them around the special delimiters to improve readability. The specific use of special delimiters will be fully discussed as the control cards on which they are required are described.

4.1.2.6 Mathematical Operators

A few of the SPSS control cards require the use of mathematical operators when constructing the specifications. These operators are used on COMPUTE and IF control cards which specify variable transformations. *Transformations* refers to the construction of new variables or alterations of the values of existing ones by logical or mathematical manipulations or by a combination of variables. The COMPUTE and IF control cards are not discussed in the primer, but a full description of their use can be found in the SPSS manual.

4.1.3 SUMMARY OF GENERAL RULES FOR CONTROL-CARD PREPARATION

1 *Control words* must be spelled and spaced correctly, exactly as given in the primer.
2 *Names* may consist of from one to eight characters, the first of which must be alphabetic.
3 *Names* must be composed of letters and/or numbers. No special characters may be used.
4 *Values* are numbers and may consist of either integers or decimal numbers.[1]
5 *Keywords* must be spelled and spaced exactly as presented in the text.
6 *Individual names, keywords, and values* must consist of contiguous characters. That is, they may have no imbedded blanks or other delimiters.
7 *Individual names, keywords, and values* must be contained on a single punched card. They may *not* begin on one card and end on a second.
8 *Labels,* unlike the other elements, can be split between cards. They may not, however, exceed their maximum specified length. Some labels may be composed of any valid characters, but certain types of labels have some specific exceptions, as will be discussed in later chapters.
9 *Names, keywords, values, and labels* must be separated from one another by delimiters.
10 *Common delimiters* (i.e., blanks and commas) are used to separate names, values, keywords, and labels unless one of the *special delimiters* (e.g., parentheses, slash, or equals sign) is specified.
11 Additional *common delimiters* may be inserted between names, values, keywords, labels, and special delimiters to improve readability.
12 If the specification field requires more than one control card, it may be continued in columns 16 through 80 of succeeding cards. Columns 1 through 15 of these continuation cards must, however, be left blank.

---

[1]You may also use alphabetic values under certain circumstances, but they require special procedures. See the SPSS manual for details.

Additional rules governing the construction of individual control cards are to be found under the detailed descriptions of the SPSS commands.

The general rules listed above are demonstrated by the following three example MISSING VALUES cards:

```
1            16
MISSING VALUES SEX RACE (9)/ AGE(98 99)
MISSING VALUES SEXRACE (9)/ AGE(9899)
MISING VALUE SEX,RACE(9)/ AGE(98,99)
```

MISSING VALUES cards are used to tell SPSS which values are to be treated as missing data codes for each variable. The first of these example cards is correct. Each variable name is separated by at least one blank and/or comma. The values and keywords are also separated from other elements by blanks, except where special delimiters are employed. Note that special delimiters may or may not be separated from other elements by blanks.

The second MISSING VALUES card is incorrect and demonstrates some common violations of the rules. The variable names SEX and RACE have no delimiter between them, so it is impossible for SPSS to recognize them as separate names. This violation is fatal (unless a variable called SEXRACE happens to exist) and would result in an error message and termination of the run. In addition, the intended values 98 and 99 for the AGE variable have no common delimiter between them and, hence, would be recognized as the single value 9899. This is not a fatal error, but it would certainly produce undesired results. Such an error can be costly and can easily go undetected. A value of 9899 is very acceptable to SPSS (even if it never occurs in the data), and SPSS has no way of knowing that this was not the intention.

Finally, the last card would cause a fatal error, because the control words are misspelled and the specification field was begun before column 16. A detailed description of the MISSING VALUES command will be given in Chap. 5.

At each stage of processing, the SPSS system checks the syntax and order of all control cards for errors. If an error is encountered, an error number is printed below the offending control card. The remaining control cards of that processing step are also checked for further errors. The run is then terminated with a list of the error numbers encountered and a description of each. This information will help you locate the exact error.

4.2 NOTATION USED IN PRESENTING CONTROL-CARD FORMATS

In the following chapters, we will use some special notation in presenting the control-card formats. This notation will help you distinguish between keywords and descriptive phrases. It will point out places where you have a choice among keywords or types of specifications, and it will set off optional parts of the specifications.

For instance, specifications presented in brackets [ ] are optional and may be omitted if not needed.

Brace marks { } denote portions of the instruction which can take one or more element, name list, or keyword. They indicate that you are to make a choice among the alternatives. Two examples of how the alternatives are presented are:

$$\left\{\begin{array}{c} \text{CARD} \\ \text{or} \\ \text{TAPE} \\ \text{or} \\ \text{DISK} \\ \text{or} \\ \text{OTHER} \end{array}\right\} \quad \text{or} \quad \left\{\begin{array}{c} \text{variable name} \\ \text{or} \\ \text{variable list} \end{array}\right\}$$

In the first example, a choice is to be made among four specific keywords. The second example illustrates a choice among two styles of specification.

Keywords and control words are presented in *full capitals*. Whenever you encounter elements in full capitals, you must copy them exactly as presented. When alternatives are presented, you must make a choice.

When specifications are presented in lower case, you are to replace them with the proper elements. If, for example, you see the notation (value list), you should insert the desired value list within the parentheses, as explained in the instructions for that control card.

The special delimiters [(,), /, and =] are presented where they should appear in the specification field. The common delimiters, however, are not always presented.

5

DEFINING AN SPSS SYSTEM FILE

Informing SPSS about the nature of your data is an important step in preparing your data for analysis. The task of naming the variables, specifying their locations on the data cards, identifying missing values, providing labels, and a few related operations is called *defining the SPSS system file*. The control cards needed to describe the data for the system file are called *data-definition cards*. SPSS uses the data-definition cards to create the system file described in Sec. 3.4. After you have defined the file, you will be able to recode variables and request statistical analyses.

As you read through this chapter, keep in mind that you must use data-definition cards whenever you are supplying raw input data to SPSS. *Raw input data* are any data on cards, tape, or other storage media which have not been previously converted by SPSS into a system file. The data-definition cards are prepared and entered only once for any given file unless changes are desired on some later run. You are required to enter the data-definition cards and raw input data at the same time (although the data may be on some other medium, such as tape or disk). SPSS then converts the data into a special system file according to your instructions and makes this file available for immediate statistical analysis.

If you include a SAVE FILE instruction, the system file will be permanently stored on a tape or disk. The saved file can then be used at a future time for further analyses without requiring new data-definition instructions. This facility saves computing time and makes it easier for you to repeatedly access your data.

5.1 FILE NAME CARD

The FILE NAME card assigns a name to the system file you are creating. A *file name* is an SPSS-type name that refers to a system file. It enables you to retrieve your system file at a future time for further analyses. As with all SPSS names, the file name can be composed of from one to eight characters, provided that the first character is a letter and no blanks or special characters are used. Some examples are: FILE1, CRIMESTD, VOTEDATA, and SEPT1374.

The FILE NAME card begins with the control words FILE NAME starting in column 1. You then enter a file name and label of your choice in the specification field. The file name and label must be separated by a common delimiter (comma or blank). A *file label* is any information up to 64 characters in length. It is printed on the output as partial documentation of the system file. You may use any characters to create the label, including the common and special delimiters. SPSS prints the label exactly as you have entered it on the card. Both the file name and the file label are stored with the system file and appear on all printed output generated from that file.

The general format of the FILE NAME card is as follows:

1	16
FILE NAME	file name [file label]

Three examples that illustrate the use of the FILE NAME card are:

```
1               16
FILE NAME       FILE1, FIRST FILE FROM DR. SMITH'S INFLATION STUDY
FILE NAME       CRIMESTD  CINCINNATI CRIME STUDY (SEPT., 1974)
FILE NAME       SEPT1374
```

5.2 DATA LIST CARD

The DATA LIST card defines the type, location, and width (number of columns) of each of the variables being entered into SPSS. The card informs SPSS whether the data are in fixed-column or binary format, the number of records per case, the name and location of each variable, and whether any variables are of alphabetic type. The control words DATA LIST appear in the control field with the rest of the information coming in the specification field. Since the DATA LIST specifications are very important, but somewhat complicated, we will discuss each part in detail while gradually putting together the full set of specifications. Because binary input data and alphabetic variables are not normally encountered by beginners, they are not discussed in the primer, although they are covered fully in the SPSS manual.

5.2.1 SPECIFYING FIXED-COLUMN INPUT DATA

Usually data are supplied to SPSS in a fixed-column format. As was discussed in Sec. 3.3, this is where each variable is punched in the same card and column location for each case. It is "fixed" in the sense that if we know that the variable SEX is in the tenth column of card 2, we can always find the individual's sex in column 10 of card 2.

If your data are punched in fixed-column form, you begin the DATA LIST specification with the keyword FIXED. The beginning of the card would then look like this:

1	16
DATA LIST	FIXED

Immediately following this first keyword, you punch the number of physical cards or records per case. Recall that each case may have more than one card. This is the point where you tell SPSS how many cards to expect for each case. This number must be enclosed in parentheses and followed by a slash. For example, you would indicate 10 data cards per case as follows:

```
1               16
DATA LIST       FIXED (10)/
```

Note that one or more blanks may appear on either side of the parentheses and between the parentheses and the number, although none are required. Such blanks are optional and are normally used to improve readability. The slash informs SPSS that this specification is ended and another one follows.

If you have only one data card per case, the number may be omitted. Thus, the following two examples are equivalent:

```
1               16
DATA LIST       FIXED(1)/
DATA LIST       FIXED/
```

The rules for the first DATA LIST specification can be summarized in the following general format.

```
1               16
DATA LIST       FIXED[(number of cards or records per case)]/
```

5.2.2 VARIABLE LISTS

The remaining specifications on the DATA LIST card are used to name the input variables and to identify their locations on the data cards. Before learning how this is done, you will need to know something about "variable lists" and how they are used in SPSS.

Very simply, a *variable list* is a series of variable names. On the DATA LIST card, the variable list names the variables that will be read from your raw input data. This is the means by which SPSS learns the names you wish to use in referring to your variables.

Every variable to be used by SPSS must have a unique name. The usual rules for names apply as described in Sec. 4.1.2.1.[1] Examples of naming variables for an entire data set are given in the two codebooks appearing in Appendix A. The second column of the codebook contains the name used for each variable when the data were placed into SPSS system files by the authors.

The name you give to a variable is arbitrary, but it must not be the same as any other variable name in the same file. You will find it helpful to select names that suggest the nature of the variables. For example, suppose that the variables being used in a particular study are a person's age, sex, income, occupation, and level of education. Obvious descriptive names for these variables would be AGE, SEX, INCOME, OCCUP, and EDUC. You may use nonsense names or names created out of numbers, but these are not generally recommended. The great advantages of meaningful names are that you quickly learn to associate them with the corresponding variables and that you are less likely to misspell them.

Often you will find that you have a raw data set with many more variables than are needed for the current analyses. In this situation, you do not have to name all of the variables. You need to name only those variables you wish to transfer from the raw data into the SPSS system file. Any unnamed variables are ignored by SPSS.

---

[1] The following names and keywords may not be used as variable names, as they are reserved for other uses in the SPSS language: SEQNUM, CASWGT, SUBFILE, ALL, TO, WITH, BY, SQRT, EXP, LN, SIN, COS, ATAN, RND, LG10, ABS, TRUNC, MOD10, GE, LE, GT, LT, EQ, NE, AND, OR, and NOT.

Normally, the sequence in which variable names appear on the DATA LIST card will be the same as their order in the raw data. As you can see in Appendix A, the first four variables in the Communities Study are COMCODE, CARDN01, MEDSCH, and MEDFINC. Consequently, on the DATA LIST card COMCODE is named first, CARDN01 is named second, MEDSCH third, and MEDFINC fourth. Although this is the normal procedure, you may find it desirable to name variables in some other sequence. Sec. 5.2.3 explains how and when this may be done. Thus, the first four variables from the Communities Study could have appeared on the DATA LIST card in the order MEDSCH, CARDN01, MEDFINC, COMCODE. Alternatively, only MEDSCH and MEDFINC need be named if you feel that COMCODE and CARDN01 are not needed in the system file.

5.2.3 ASSOCIATING VARIABLE NAMES WITH DATA LOCATIONS

In addition to specifying the variable names, the DATA LIST card is used to link each variable name with the location of that variable on the raw-input-data cards. If the variable COMCODE is located in columns 1 through 3, this is communicated through the DATA LIST specifications. The format of these specifications is somewhat complicated but very logical. The sections below describe each part of the specifications in detail.

To begin with, let us assume we are going to read in only the first variable from the American Small Communities Study. Because there is only one card per case, the following instruction would completely communicate our desire.

```
1               16
DATA LIST       FIXED (1)/ 1 COMCODE 1-3
```

The second specification (i.e., 1 COMCODE 1-3) names the variable and identifies its location on the data card. The number 1 immediately *following* the slash denotes the card on which the following group of variables is located. In this example, there is only one card per case, but the card number must still be supplied. (When there are several cards per case, this number is all the more important.) The card number is followed by a common delimiter, a variable name, and then another common delimiter. After this the range of column locations used by the variable is given. In this instance, COMCODE starts in column 1 and ends in column 3. The two column locations are separated by a dash, and the dash may be surrounded by common delimiters if desired (i.e., 1-3 and 1 − 3 and 1,−,3 are all equivalent).

Let us now expand this example to include the next three variables listed in the codebook. The appropriate DATA LIST would be

```
1               16
DATA LIST       FIXED(1)/ 1 COMCODE 1-3, CARDN01 5, MEDSCH 7-9 (1), MEDFINC 11-14
```

The first thing to notice is that the card number appears only after a slash. You must not repeat the card number for variables located *on the same card*. Next, notice that each variable is followed by its column location. CARDN01 is located in column 5 of the data card. Because it is one column wide, only that single column needs to be given. Columns 4 and 6 happen to be blank on these data cards, so they are skipped. MEDSCH occupies three columns—7, 8, and 9—so both the beginning and ending columns must be given. The same is true for MEDFINC, which occupies four columns (11–14).

When the values of a variable are fractional numbers, you may punch them on the data cards without the decimal point, provided you always use the same number of decimal digits. For instance, the variable MEDSCH takes on the values 8.6, 8.6, 9.5, 9.4, and 12.6 years of median education for the first five cities in the COMSTUDY data file. These values were punched on the data cards as 86, 86, 95, 94, and 126. The omission of the decimal point means that only three columns are needed for this variable instead of four, and that less work is involved in punching the values. If we have a means of telling the computer where to insert the decimal point, the correct values can be retrieved at the time the data are read. In the SPSS language, this is done on the DATA LIST card by punching the number of implied decimal digits, enclosed in parentheses, after the column location of the variable. In this example, the specification MEDSCH 7–9 (1) is appropriate. It says that the decimal point should be reinserted so that there is one decimal digit to the right of it. The number in parentheses is called the *implied decimal indicator.*

If a decimal point is present on the data card, it is used in the position where it is found regardless of the value of the implied decimal indicator. Therefore, the values 9.1 and 091 would both be interpreted as 9.1 years of education, when the variable MEDSCH is read. If the value .68 is punched on the card *with the decimal point,* it too would be acceptable. In this instance, it would be interpreted as .68 years of education despite an implied decimal indicator of (1). (Of course, such a value is unlikely for this variable, because it is so low.) Remember, however, that a punched decimal point takes a column and that the entire value must fit within the space allotted. Consequently, it would be improper to punch the four characters 8.23 as a value for MEDSCH, since only three columns have been allotted.

If no implied decimal indicator is given for a variable, the decimal point is placed at the end of the number unless a decimal point has been punched on the data card. Thus, the four-column value 4231 for the variable MEDFINC would be interpreted as 4,231.0.

The column locations and implied decimal indicator are separated from the next variable in the list by a common delimiter. The last variable name and its associated columns need not be followed by a slash.

The complete DATA LIST command for the American Small Communities Study data is as follows.

```
1               16
DATA LIST       FIXED(1)/1 COMCODE 1-3, CARDNO1 5, MEDSCH 7-9 (1), MEDFINC 11-14,
                PTGOHS PTAGRI PTMANU PTTERTRY 15-30 (1), POP60 POPLAT 31-44,
                PTCHNG 45-49 (1), SPISOL 50-51, WHTCOLAR 52-55 (1), LIFE TIME
                NEWSWEEK READDIG 56-67, HRSWORK GOVSELCT CONELECT PARTISAN
                PARTROLE 68-72
```

As you can see, several variables do not have column numbers following the variable name. This may be done when there are two or more adjacent variables of the same width and having the same number of implied decimal digits. An example is the specification

PTGOHS PTAGRI PTMANU PTTERTRY 15–30 (1)

This says that the four variables equally divide up the space between columns 15 through 30, inclusive, and that each has one implied decimal digit. An equivalent specification would look like this:

PTGOHS 15–18(1), PTAGRI 19–22(1), PTMANU 23–26(1), PTTERTRY 27–30(1)

When the shorter notation is used, the range of column numbers denotes the beginning column of the first variable and the ending column of the last variable. This notation may be used only when the variables are of the same width.

To illustrate additional features of the DATA LIST card we need a more complicated data set. Therefore, imagine a data set containing many variables and requiring four cards per case. We want to read in only 15 of the variables, however. These variables, their locations, and the number of implied decimal digits are listed in Table 5.1. The following is an appropriate DATA LIST card for these variables.

TABLE 5.1   Card Locations of 15 Example Variables

Card	Column(s)	Variable name	Number of implied decimal digits	Missing value(s)
1	26	EYECOLOR	0	0, 8, 9
	27	BALDNESS	0	0, 8, 9
	28	ANEMIA	0	0, 8, 9
2	5–7	SCORE1	2	9.99
	8–10	SCORE2	2	9.99
	11–13	SCORE3	2	0
	14–16	SCORE4	2	0
	57	HAYFEVER	0	0, 8, 9
	63	ALGYCATS	0	0, 8, 9
	64	ALGYDOGS	0	0, 8, 9
4	30–31	SCALE15	0	0, −1
	32–33	SCALE16	0	0, 8, 9
	34–35	SCALE17	0	0
	48–49	HRTBEAT	0	None
	69–71	BLDPRESS	0	0

```
1              16
DATA LIST      FIXED(4)/1 EYECOLOR BALDNESS ANEMIA 26-28/ 2 SCORE1, SCORE2,
               SCORE3, SCORE4  5-16 (2), HAYFEVER 57, ALGYCATS 63,
               ALGYDOGS 64/ 4 SCALE15, SCALE16, SCALE17  30-35,
               HRTBEAT 48-49, BLDPRESS 69-71
```

Here, the first specification tells the SPSS program that the data are in fixed-column format with four cards per case. The second specification names and locates the variables desired from the first card. There are three adjacent one-column variables with no implied decimal digits. EYECOLOR is in column 26, BALDNESS is in column 27, and ANEMIA is in column 28.

The next specification identifies the variables to be read from the second card. Notice that it is necessary to start a new specification with the card number 2 coming immediately after the slash which ended the previous specification. Variables SCORE1, SCORE2, SCORE3, and SCORE4 are located in columns 5 through 16, which is a total of 12 columns (16 − 5 + 1 = 12). This means that each of these variables is three columns wide with SCORE1 in columns 5 through 7, SCORE2 in columns 8 through 10, etc. This specification also tells SPSS that each of these four variables has two implied decimal digits.

When the remaining variables from the second card have been listed (i.e., HAYFEVER, ALGYCATS, and ALGYDOGS), a slash is used to end the specification. This slash is followed by the number 4 to denote that the remaining variables are to be read from the fourth card. Because no variables are desired from the third card, no reference is made to it.

Two rules relating to the handling of multicard cases are illustrated in this example. First, all variables desired from a single card must be listed together in the same specification with the card number appearing immediately after the slash which ended the previous specification. Second, the *card* specifications must be in sequential order. If no variables are desired from a given card, that card is not referenced.

Another feature of the DATA LIST instruction is that the variables need not be named in the same sequence in which they physically appear on the raw data cards. For instance, if we wanted to store HRTBEAT and BLDPRESS *before* SCALE15, SCALE16, and SCALE17 *in the system file*, the specification for the fourth card could have been entered as

4 HRTBEAT 48–49, BLDPRESS 69–71, SCALE15, SCALE16, SCALE17 30–35

These five variables would then appear in the SPSS system file in the sequence HRTBEAT, BLDPRESS, SCALE15, SCALE16, and SCALE17. This reordering of variables is permitted only for variables punched on the same card in the raw data file. HRTBEAT and BLDPRESS could not be named before EYECOLOR, because EYECOLOR is located on an earlier data card. Although variables on the same card may be named out of order, the cards themselves must be referenced in ascending order. While it is possible to name variables out of order, this procedure is not recommended unless you have a good reason for using it.

The DATA LIST instruction also allows you to refer to the same card columns more than once. This is particularly useful when a specific variable is a composite of two or more pieces of information. Suppose each case of a raw-input-data file represents a school, and the first five columns of the single card for each case contain a school identification number: columns 1 and 2 identify the state in which the school is located; columns 3 and 4, the county; and column 5 is the school's sequence number within the county. The school identification number plus its three subsections can all be read as separate variables in this fashion:

```
1                 16
DATA LIST         FIXED/1 SCHOOLID 1-5   STATE 1-2   COUNTY 3-4   SCHSEQ 5/
```

The use of the DATA LIST card for fixed-column, numeric data can be summarized in the following general format.

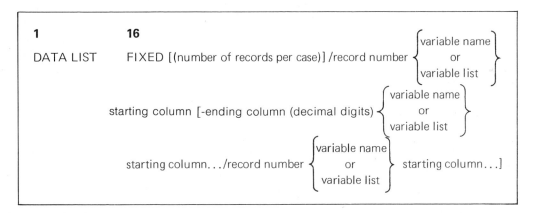

Here, "record number" has been used instead of "card number," because the same format applies to data stored as records on a tape or disk. (A card is a single "record" in a card file.) If any of the variables are to be read in alphabetic mode, a minor addition is required, as explained in the SPSS manual.

5.2.4 ALTERNATIVE TO THE DATA LIST CARD

The SPSS language allows an alternative to the DATA LIST card for the purpose of naming and identifying the location of variables. This is the joint use of the VARIABLE LIST and INPUT FORMAT instructions. The chief advantage of the VARIABLE LIST and INPUT FORMAT procedure is that it is easier to use when the raw data are arranged in a repetitive format but where adjacent variables are not of the same width. For more information about this procedure, see the SPSS manual.

5.3 INPUT MEDIUM CARD

The INPUT MEDIUM card informs the SPSS system of the *medium* you are using to supply raw data. The control words INPUT MEDIUM are followed by one of four keywords depending upon the location of your data. The keyword CARD is used when the data are being entered on cards along with SPSS control cards. The keyword TAPE is used when the data reside on a computer tape; the keyword DISK is used when your data reside on a disk file; and the keyword OTHER is used when the data are on some other device available at your installation. The general format of the INPUT MEDIUM card is

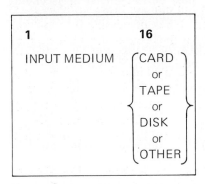

The keyword CARD tells SPSS that your data cases will be entered on cards along with the SPSS control cards. In this situation, the data cases and the SPSS control cards are entered into the computer together via the card reader. The keyword CARD was originally chosen for this purpose because most SPSS control "cards" were actually punched on physical cards; so when the data cases accompanied them, they too were on cards. It is becoming more and more common for computer users to enter their SPSS control "cards" from a remote keyboard terminal such as a teletype. When you do this and when you also enter the data cases from the terminal with the SPSS control "cards," you just specify the keyword CARD in the INPUT MEDIUM instruction. In such instances the keyword CARD merely indicates that the data cases *accompany* the SPSS control cards, not that they are actually punched on physical cards.

5.4 N OF CASES CARD

The N OF CASES card simply informs SPSS of the number of data cases to expect. The general format of the card is

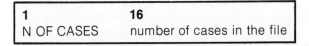

The control words N OF CASES are followed by the actual number of cases. If, for example, you have a file containing 1,008 cases, the N OF CASES card would appear as

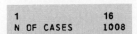

You should be careful that the number supplied here is the exact number of *cases*. When there are multiple cards per case, you will have, of course, more cards than cases. For instance, if your data require four cards per case, you must supply 4,032 *data cards* while informing SPSS that you have 1,008 *cases*.

5.5 MISSING VALUES CARD

Very often in social science research some of the cases in a file do not have complete information for every variable. Usually, a special value is punched on the data cards to indicate the absence of information. Other values may be considered by you as inappropriate or undesirable for use in the statistical analyses. In any of these situations, the designated values are referred to as "missing values." The SPSS system allows you to specify up to three missing values for each variable, so that a file containing cases with incomplete data may still be conveniently processed.

If, for example, you have a file composed of the variables RACE, AGE, and IN-COME and some cases are missing information on one or more of these variables, you would assign certain values to represent the different types of missing information. RACE would probably require one missing value, 0, for those cases in which the respondent's race was not reported. For the variables INCOME (coded in thousands of dollars) and AGE, you might desire to preserve more detailed information about why the cases are missing. In this instance, you might choose the value 98 for those persons who refused to answer and 99 for those cases in which the interviewer had seemingly forgotten to ascertain the respondent's age or income. In addition, you might reserve another value, perhaps 88, on the variable INCOME for those persons who did not know their annual income.

When coding data, you must be careful to choose missing values which are distinct from real values. For example, 98 and 99 are suitable for missing data codes for the variable AGE only if you are sure that none of the respondents are actually 98 or 99 years old. That is a fairly safe assumption, of course, but obviously the value 40 would generally be a poor choice as a missing data code for the variable AGE.

When a file containing missing data is processed, the values which have been designated as missing are checked against the values on each case as it is processed. When a missing value is encountered on a case, that case may be treated in a number of different ways depending upon the statistical procedure being used and the missing-data options selected. Descriptions of the missing-data options available in any procedure are discussed in later chapters.

Values to be designated as missing are defined by the MISSING VALUES card and stored with the data cases in an SPSS system file. An appropriate MISSING VALUES card for the three variables we just discussed would look like this:

```
1               16
MISSING VALUES RACE(0)/ AGE(98,99)/ INCOME (88,98,99)/
```

The MISSING VALUES card contains the control words MISSING VALUES followed by the variable name or list of variable names for which one to three missing values are to be declared. The variable name or variable list is in turn followed by the missing value or values that apply to those variables. These missing values must be enclosed within a set of parentheses. Another variable name or variable list may then follow this set of values; however, a slash must be placed (as a delimiter) between the missing values list and the second variable name or variable list. This second list of variable names is again followed by the missing value or values that apply to these variables. The process can be repeated until all the desired missing values have been defined. Alternately, you may define a new MISSING VALUES card for each variable or set of variables. The general format of the MISSING VALUES card is

```
1               16
MISSING VALUES { variable name
                     or          } (missing values)/ { variable name
                                                           or          } (missing values)
                  variable list                         variable list
```

TABLE 5.2 Correspondence between Variable Names and Sequential Position of the Variables

Position of variable in system file	Corresponding variable name	Position of variable in system file	Corresponding variable name
1	EYECOLOR	9	ALGYCATS
2	BALDNESS	10	ALGYDOGS
3	ANEMIA	11	SCALE15
4	SCORE1	12	SCALE16
5	SCORE2	13	SCALE17
6	SCORE3	14	HRTBEAT
7	SCORE4	15	BLDPRESS
8	HAYFEVER		

The variables named on the MISSING VALUES card must be variables which have been previously defined.[1] When two or more variables in a file are to take the same missing values, a *list* of variable names can be entered onto the MISSING VALUES card. This list of variable names will cause the same missing values to be declared for each of these variables, thus reducing the amount of card preparation. The variable list is entered onto the MISSING VALUES card by one of two notations, depending upon the sequential location of the variables in the system file.

Remember that SPSS stores your variables in the order in which they are named on the DATA LIST card. Table 5.2 illustrates this sequence for the variables given in Table 5.1. The variables ANEMIA and SCORE1 are "adjacent," because they are stored next to one another in the system file. ANEMIA and HAYFEVER, however, are not adjacent, because other variables are located between them.

Where three or more *adjacent* variables are to take the same missing values, the variable *names* may be entered onto the card by using the *inclusive* TO *notation. When three or more consecutive variables are being named, you need to name only the first and last with the keyword* TO *between them.* This is illustrated by the following example using variables from Table 5.1:

EYECOLOR TO ANEMIA

EYECOLOR and ANEMIA are variables which have been previously defined, and EYECOLOR precedes ANEMIA in the sequence of variables stored in the system file. All variables between EYECOLOR and ANEMIA (i.e., EYECOLOR, BALDNESS, and ANEMIA) are to take the same missing values. This notation enables you to simultaneously define missing values for large numbers of adjacent variables.

When two or more *nonadjacent* variables are to take the same missing values, the variable names are entered onto the MISSING VALUES card in the following manner:

SCORE3, SCORE4, SCALE17, BLDPRESS

Variables SCORE3, SCORE4, SCALE17, and BLDPRESS are variables which take the same missing values, but only two of them are adjacent.

These two notations may be freely intermixed, producing a list of variable names of the following type:

EYECOLOR TO ANEMIA, HAYFEVER TO ALGYDOGS, SCALE16

A variable name or variable list is followed by the missing value or values (up to

---

[1]In most cases, these will be variables which have been defined on the DATA LIST card. However, new variables may be defined by means of variable transformations (as described in the SPSS manual), and these variables may also take missing values.

three) to be associated with the variables. The missing value or values are enclosed within parentheses and must be separated from one another by one or more common delimiters. For example, (0, 8, 9) or (0, −1) or (9.99) specify sets of three, two, and one missing values, respectively.

The missing value(s) will then be followed by a slash, which may be followed by another variable name or variable list and the associated missing values. This may be repeated (i.e., variable list, missing values, slash; variable list, missing values, slash; etc.) until all the desired missing values have been defined. Variables that have no missing values are simply not included in the list of variables on the MISSING VALUES list.

The following sample MISSING VALUES card demonstrates the general format of the card and the types of variable lists which can be used. The variables and missing values are those given in Table 5.1.

```
1              16
MISSING VALUES SCALE16, EYECOLOR TO ANEMIA (0,8,9)/ SCORE3, SCORE4,
               BLDPRESS, SCALE17 (0)/ SCALE15 (0,-1)/ HAYFEVER
               TO ALGYDOGS (0,8,9)/ SCORE1  SCORE2 (9.99)/
```

Note that the variables need not be in any particular order except when the TO notation is used. In addition, variables with the same missing values need not be grouped into a single list, although this is usually easiest. Variables should be named only once on the MISSING VALUES card. If you should happen to list a variable twice, the second set of values will *completely replace* the first set regardless of the number of values involved.

5.6 VAR LABELS CARD

The SPSS system permits you to associate a label with any or all the variables in your file. A variable name such as MEDSCH has some meaning to people who are very familiar with the data file. You and others, however, will find tables using this variable easier to understand if a label is also printed which says, "median school years for population over 25." Whenever a variable having one of these labels is used in a statistical procedure of the sort that prints labels, the label is printed on the output from that procedure. This can be very helpful to you, because the labels provide permanent and full documentation of your tables and other calculations. The variable labels, like all other information entered on the data-definition cards, may be permanently stored with the data as an SPSS system file.

The cards used to enter these extended variable labels contain the control words VAR LABELS in the control field. The first entry in the specification field is a *single variable name*. The variable name is then followed by a common delimiter and a label up to 40 characters (including imbedded blanks) in length. A slash follows the label and may be succeeded by a second variable name and its associated label. This order of variable name, variable label, slash is repeated until all the desired variable labels have been defined. Alternately, you may define each variable label on a separate VAR LABELS card. The general format of the VAR LABELS card is

```
1              16

VAR LABELS     variable name, variable label/variable name, variable label/,...,
               variable name, variable label
```

A variable label may apply to only one variable, and a variable must have been previously defined before a label can be assigned to it. The order in which variables are assigned labels is not important. A variable label may be up to 40 characters in length, and may be composed of any valid printing characters with the exception of [/], [(], and [)]. The specifications on the VAR LABELS card may continue from one physical card to the next until all the desired labels have been defined. Card columns 1 to 15 of all but the first card must, however, remain blank. Variable labels, like all other labels, need not be contained on a single card. You will eliminate unnecessary blanks from a label beginning on one physical card and continuing on the next by entering the label up to the eightieth column and beginning on the sixteenth column of the next card. It is usually easier to correct mistakes, however, if only one variable name and label is given per physical card, as illustrated in Appendix A. The following is an example of a VAR LABELS card:

```
1                16
VAR LABELS       EYECOLOR, COLOR OF EYES/BALDNESS, IS PATIENT BALD?/
                 SCORE2, AVERAGE SCORE ON S-J TEST/ SCALE 16,
                 REACTION TO POLLEN, CATS, & DOGS/
```

5.7 VALUE LABELS CARD

You may also assign labels to the values of any or all the variables in your file. These are called value labels, and they are automatically printed in appropriate places whenever present. Such labels are particularly helpful and attractive in documenting output from simple and crosstabulated frequency distributions. The subsequent chapters contain sample printouts which show the use made of value labels.

Value labels are defined with the VALUE LABELS card, and once prepared, these labels may be stored with the data in an SPSS system file. The control field contains the control words VALUE LABELS beginning in column 1. You then enter the variable name or list of variable names for which a set of value labels are to be defined in the specification field. This is followed by a value enclosed in parentheses and a label up to 20 characters in length. The next value and its label follow. This is repeated until all the value labels desired for the variable(s) have been entered. You can enter additional sets of value labels for other variables by ending the first set with a slash, entering the next variable name or names, and repeating the procedure over again for the new variable(s). The general format of the card is

```
1                16
VALUE LABELS     { variable name
                     or          } (value1) label1 (value2) label2 ... (valuen) labeln/
                   variable list

                 [ { variable name
                       or          } (value1) label1 (value2) label2 ... (valuen) labeln/ ]
                     variable list
```

Variable names are entered in a manner identical to that used in the MISSING VALUES card. The same labels may be assigned to the same values of a number of different variables. This may be particularly useful when you have a number of variables which share the same coding schemes and when the values have identical interpretations. Some examples are given further below.

The variable name or list of names is followed by a single value enclosed within parentheses. The value is followed by a label up to 20 characters in length. The label may be composed of any valid printing characters with the exceptions of the slash [/], the left parenthesis [(], and the right parenthesis [)], which may not be used because of their function as delimiters.

Value labels are reported on output exactly as they are spaced and spelled. A label begins with the first non-blank character following the right parenthesis. It continues until a left parenthesis is encountered or 20 character spaces have been encountered (including imbedded blanks), whichever comes first. Each value label is followed by the next value for which a label is to be defined. You may label all the values for a variable or, if you desire, only selected values. The last value label defined for a variable or list of variables may be followed by a slash if value labels for other variables are to be defined on that card. The next variable name or list of names follows the slash and then their value labels in exactly the same manner as before.

The following sample VALUE LABELS card demonstrates how the VALUE LABELS card should be prepared.

```
1              16
VALUE LABELS   INCOME (1) UNDER $1000 (2) $1000-1999 (3) $2000-3999
               (4) $4000-5999 (5) $6000-7999 (6)$8000-9999
               (7) $10000-14999 (8) $15000 AND OVER
               (9) REFUSED TO ANSWER (0) DON'T KNOW/
               ITEM1 TO ITEM10 (5)AGREE STRONGLY (4) AGREE (3) NEUTRAL
               (2) DISAGREE (1) DISAGREE STRONGLY (9) REFUSED TO ANSWER
               (0) DON'T KNOW/
               EDUCATN (1) NO EDUCATION (2) PRIMARY OR LESS
               (3) SOME SECONDARY (4) GRAD SECONDARY (5) SOME COLLEGE
               (6) COLLEGE GRAD OR MORE/
```

Labels, unlike any of the other types of elements, may be split between two physical cards. You will eliminate undesired internal blanks from labels beginning on one card and continuing on the next by entering the label up to the eightieth column and beginning immediately in the sixteenth column of the next card. You may define value labels for all variables on a single VALUE LABELS card and its continuations. Alternately, a new card may be prepared for the value labels associated with a specific variable or set of variables. However, a variable name may be referenced *only once* on a VALUE LABELS card during a given computer run.

5.8 RULES COVERING THE ORDER OF THE DATA-DEFINITION CARDS

All the data-definition cards to be discussed in the primer have now been defined. Table 5.3 lists the control fields for these data-definition cards. Once these cards have been prepared, the SPSS system can obtain all the necessary and any optional information to be used in processing the data. The internal order or sequence of most of the data-definition cards is quite free, and, with the exceptions of the following four rules, the cards may be placed in any order you desire.

1 In the initial file-generating runs, all data-definition cards are grouped together as one set of cards in the control-card deck. The combined set of data-definition cards always appears near the beginning of the control-card deck. (Exact deck placement will be discussed in Sec. 7.3.)
2 The FILE NAME card is normally the first data-definition card when it is used.
3 The DATA LIST, the INPUT MEDIUM, and the N OF CASES cards must come next, *in that order*.
4 The remaining data-definition cards are inserted into the control-card deck next and can be in any order you desire.

The order of the control fields presented in Table 5.3 below reflects the above four rules. "Conditional" status means that the card is required under certain conditions as mentioned in Table 5.3 under "Remarks." "Required" cards are, of course, required in all file-defining runs, and "optional" cards are used at your discretion.

TABLE 5.3 Status of Data-Definition Cards

Card status	Control field	Remarks
Conditional	FILE NAME	Required if an SPSS system file is to be generated.
Required†	DATA LIST	
Required	INPUT MEDIUM	
Required†	N OF CASES	
Optional	MISSING VALUES	
Optional	VAR LABELS	
Optional	VALUE LABELS	

†Alternatives not described in the primer may be used in place of the DATA LIST and N OF CASES cards.

5.9 SAVING AND RETRIEVING SYSTEM FILES

So far in this chapter, we have presented the essential SPSS language instructions for creating a system file from raw input data. Once you have defined the file, you may go on to recode variables (discussed in Chap. 6), create new variables (discussed in the SPSS manual), and request statistical computations. All of this may be done in the same computer run. SPSS will perform a multitude of tasks in the same run by reusing the temporary system file (as explained in Sec. 3.4). Finally, the system file may be permanently saved on a tape, disk, or other direct-access medium by using the SAVE FILE instruction. An SPSS system file that has been saved may be retrieved for further processing with the GET FILE instruction.

5.9.1 SAVE FILE CARD

The cases, as well as all the file-defining information entered on the data-definition cards, may be retained as an SPSS system file (on a tape or disk) at the conclusion of any processing run by means of the SAVE FILE control card.[1] The SAVE FILE card causes the file which is presently being processed to be saved in the form of an SPSS system file at the conclusion of the run. Its format is

1	16
SAVE FILE	[file name, file label]

On the initial file-generating run, the card contains the control words SAVE FILE and requires no further specifications.

The optional specification field will rarely be used on file-generating runs, since the file will have already been named and labeled with the FILE NAME card. However, once you have modified the information in your file in later runs (by recoding, variable transformations, new data-defining information, etc.), you may wish to save an updated version of the system file with a new name and optional label, which can be defined directly on the SAVE FILE card.

The SAVE FILE card is inserted into the control-card deck directly in front of the FINISH card (see Sec. 7.2.2) and may be employed during any processing run. A separate file-generating run is not required. Whenever an SPSS system file is saved by means of a SAVE FILE control card, you are informed as to whether the file was suc-

---

[1]When you wish to save an SPSS system file, you must prepare a job control card for the file. The information and format required for these cards vary radically from one type of computer to another. Detailed instructions are given in Appendices E–G of the SPSS manual and on handouts available at most computer facilities.

cessfully saved and also provided with a list of the variables, the number of variables, and the number of cases contained in the new file.

5.9.2 GET FILE CARD

Once an SPSS system file has been generated and retained, the data as well as the information describing them are accessible on all subsequent runs by means of the GET FILE control card. However, neither the data nor the documenting information within an SPSS system file are unalterable. Labels and missing values may be changed, and recoding may be accomplished. (As is explained in the SPSS manual, you may even add new variables and/or cases under certain conditions.) In short, processing from an SPSS system file means that you need only concern yourself with requesting the statistical task, because the file has already been defined. The GET FILE card causes the saved file to be positioned for processing and makes all the information about the data available to SPSS.[1] Thus, it is unnecessary to resupply this information.

The card contains the control words GET FILE followed by the name of the file that has previously been generated and retained (by means of the SAVE FILE card). The name must be spelled in the same way as it was on the FILE NAME card used to define it. The general format of the GET FILE card is

1	16
GET FILE	file name

For example, to retrieve a file that was saved with the file name STUDYA the following GET FILE card would be used.

1	16
GET FILE	STUDYA

The GET FILE card is usually the first control card unless a RUN NAME card is used (see Sec. 7.2.1), in which case it comes second. The GET FILE card is then followed by recoding and transformation instructions, if needed, and any additions or modifications you may want to make to the variable labels, value labels, and missing values. These are then followed by statistical procedure cards. Several examples will be given in subsequent chapters after some of these other features have been explained.

---

[1]Just as in the case of the raw-input-data file and the output system file, a job control statement must be prepared for an input system file, and once again, the detailed instructions for the use of these operating system statements, on the three most widely available computers for which the SPSS system is implemented, are to be found in Appendices E–G of the SPSS manual.

6
RECODING VARIABLES

Situations often arise during the analysis of social science data which require you to modify the coding scheme for some variable or variables in your file. The process of changing a variable's coding scheme is called *recoding*, *transforming*, or *data modification*. A very common type of recoding is to combine several values into one. For instance, the RACE variable in the Organizational Membership Study reported in Appendix A has separate categories of Negro, Oriental, American Indian, Latin American, and Other. You might want to combine all of these into a single Nonwhite category for theoretical or practical reasons. Or you might want to collapse the age variable from separate values for each year into 15-year intervals. Another common type of recoding is merely to rearrange categories. For instance, a variable may be coded as 1 = yes, 2 = no, and 3 = maybe. You might want to change this coding scheme to 1 = yes, 2 = maybe, and 3 = no, so that the categories are in a more logical order. Transformations such as these can be easily achieved in SPSS with the RECODE instruction to be discussed in this chapter.

6.1 RECODE CARD

The RECODE card allows you to replace any value or set of values by a new value of your choice. This change remains in effect throughout the SPSS run and may be preserved for future use by creating a permanently saved file with the SAVE FILE instruction. Any modifications produced through the RECODE card do not change the *original* data source, however. If the RECODE card is used during an initial file-defining run, the raw-input-data file is unaffected. Similarly, if the data are already in a *permanently* saved system file and are being accessed through the GET FILE command, that system file is not changed.

40

The RECODE card begins with the control word RECODE. The specification field contains a variable name, or list of names, for which one set of recoding specifications are to apply. The variable name or list of variable names is in turn followed by the recoding specifications. The RECODE card, like most other SPSS cards, may be continued on successive cards if the entire statement cannot be completed on the first physical card. When this is the case, columns 1 through 15 of succeeding cards are left blank, and the rest of the statement is entered in columns 16 through 80 of as many cards as required.

When you want to recode more than one variable by the same set of recoding specifications, you may list the variables as you would do on the MISSING VALUES and VALUE LABELS cards. Thus, you can enter adjacent and nonadjacent variables onto the RECODE card by the following types of notation (these variables are from the ORGSTUDY file):

FRATMEM, VETMEM, FARMEM

UNIONMEM TO SCHOLMEM

FRATMEM, UNIONMEM TO SCHOLMEM, VETMEM, FARMEM

In these examples, the shorthand notation UNIONMEM TO SCHOLMEM is used to include all the variables UNIONMEM, SPORTMEM, YOUTHMEM, and SCHOLMEM. You need not list variables in their sequential order, except within the use of the TO convention. Thus, it is acceptable to list VETMEM after SCHOLMEM as is done in the third list. A variable may be included only once in the list, however.

The general format of the RECODE card is

```
1               16
                 ⎧ variable list ⎫
 RECODE          ⎨      or       ⎬  (value list = new value) [... (value list=new value)]
                 ⎩ variable name ⎭
```

Although you still have not learned the meanings of the value list and new value specifications, the following example will give you an idea of what a complete RECODE statement looks like:

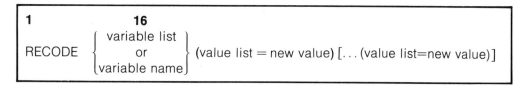

```
1               16
 RECODE          RELIG(6=2)(4, 7 THRU 9, 0=5)
```

As on most SPSS control cards, the recode instructions applying to a variable or list of variables may be followed by a slash, and a new variable or list of variables followed by its RECODE statements may then be placed after the slash. It is important to remember that RECODE specification lists are cumulative, so that it is possible on a subsequent RECODE statement to recode a previously recoded variable. More will be said about this a little later.

6.1.1 RECODE SPECIFICATION LIST

The recoding instructions are entered onto the RECODE card after the variable name or variable list by a series of parenthesized specifications of the type

(value list=new value)

The value list is one or more of the present values which you wish to have replaced by the new value on the right side of the equals sign. There are two types of alternative or combined notations you can use to enter the present values. First, you can replace a single value with a new value in the form of

(5=1)

Here, 5 is the present value and 1 is the value to which all 5s are to be recoded.

Second, you can replace a group or set of values with a single value by the following type of recoding expression:

(4,7,9=1)

In this case, all three values, 4, 7, and 9, will be replaced by 1. The three values must be separated from each other by one or more common delimiters.

Third, when you wish to replace a series of numeric values by a single value, as is often desired when converting a continuous variable into grouped categories, you may use a notation of the following type:

(32 THRU 64=1)

Here, the keyword THRU indicates that all values between and including 32 and 64 will be replaced by the value 1. Both values must be separated from the keyword THRU by one or more common delimiters.

Any of these notations may be combined to produce a list of values to be replaced by the new value at the right of the equals sign. For example, you can do this:

(1,5,22,37 THRU 68=2)

The following example, using variables from the Organizational Membership Study, illustrates how these features can be combined into a single RECODE instruction.

```
1               16
RECODE          RACE(3 THRU 8=2)/ RELIG(6=2)(4,7 THRU 9,0=5)/
                FRATMEM TO OTHMEM(0=1)(1=0)/
```

In the first specification, all the Nonwhite racial groups are being combined into category 2. Note that values not included in the specifications remain unchanged. Thus, Negroes are being indirectly combined with the other Nonwhite groups, because their category value (2) will not be changed. Similarly, Whites will remain as category 1.

The second specification, which recodes the RELIG variable, illustrates the use of multiple sets of specification lists. Multiple-specification lists are performed from left to right. As a specific case is being processed, SPSS compares its data value with the values in the value list given immediately after the variable name. If SPSS finds the case's value in the list, the designated change is made and processing is finished. If such a match is not found, the second value list is examined, and so on, until there is a match or all lists have been checked. For instance, if a case with the value 7 on the RELIG variable was being processed by the previous example RECODE instruction, SPSS would look at the specification (6=2) and find that the value 7 was not listed to the left of the equals sign. SPSS would then go to specification (4, 7 THRU 9, 0=5). Because 7 is included in this value list, SPSS would assign the new value 5 to the RELIG variable for this particular case. When no match is found in any of the lists, the original value is not changed. Thus, a case with the value 1 on the RELIG variable would retain that value, because the RECODE specification did not call for a change for the value 1. As you can see in this example, values need not be in numerical order, except where they are separated by the keyword THRU.

The last specification shows how category values may be rearranged. For variables FRATMEM TO OTHMEM, all cases which have the value 0 before recoding will have the value 1 after recoding, and vice versa. There is no confusion, because the values listed to the left of the equals sign refer to *initial* values only. Once a value has been changed, it is not reexamined within *that* specification.

A very important property to keep in mind is that the results of RECODE instructions are cumulative from one statement to the next, but that they are not cumulative within a single statement. The following examples illustrate this point for the variable FRATMEM.

```
1               16
RECODE          FRATMEM (0 = 1) (1 = 0)
RECODE          FRATMEM (0 = 1)/ FRATMEM (1 = 0)
```

On the first RECODE card, the values 0 and 1 are merely switched—cases starting with 0 are changed to 1, and vice versa. This happens because searching of the value lists stops as soon as a match is made. The second RECODE card actually consists of *two distinct* RECODE statements. The first part says to change all cases with a 0 to a 1. It says nothing at all about what to do with cases originally having a 1, so they are *not* changed. Then SPSS goes on to perform the second part of the specification, which says to *reexamine* the variable FRATMEM and change all cases with a 1 to a 0. This affects *all* cases whether the value 1 was an original data value or a newly assigned value. The final result would be that cases which originally began with 0 would be changed back to 0. Notice that the same undesired result would occur if you were to use both of the following RECODE cards in the same job.

```
1               16
RECODE          FRATMEM (0 = 1)
RECODE          FRATMEM (1 = 0)
```

When using recoding statements of the type described above, you may convert multiple-column variables into variables which contain values that are single-column integers, and vice versa. You may do this without being concerned with the number of columns occupied by the variable, because the format used for storing numbers in an SPSS file is not affected by the number of digits.

You should take special care when using the THRU convention to recode variables which contain decimal fractions as values. The internal representation of a decimal fraction may be slightly different from its external representation on the raw-input-data file. This is due to rounding errors which sometimes occur during input conversion. To ensure that all values are recoded, overlap the ranges of the value lists to be recoded. When value lists are overlapped, the variable value will be recoded to the first category into which it falls. Hence, the specification (15.3 THRU 18.15=1) (18.15 THRU 25=2) will cause all values from 15.3 up to and including 18.15 to be recoded into 1, and all values greater than 18.15 (e.g., 18.1500001) and less than or equal to 25 to be recoded to 2. If this overlapping is *not* done, you may find that certain unexpected values (like 18.1500001) have not been recoded. This would have obvious bad effects on subsequent analyses.

6.1.2 AIDS IN RECODING: THE KEYWORDS LOWEST, HIGHEST, AND ELSE

Several special keywords are available to make preparation of the RECODE cards easier. The keywords LOWEST and HIGHEST are useful when recoding continuous numeric variables into grouped categories. The keyword LOWEST refers to the lowest value of a given variable, and HIGHEST similarly refers to the highest value. The use of these two keywords will enable you to recode a variable without having complete information concerning its minimum and maximum values. An example of this use follows.

```
1               16
RECODE          VAR001(LOWEST THRU 25=1)(26 THRU 50=2)(51 THRU HIGHEST=3)
```

The keywords LOWEST and HIGHEST may be abbreviated as LO and HI, respectively. Thus, the above RECODE card could have been written:

```
1               16
RECODE          VAR001 (LO THRU 25=1)(26 THRU 50=2)(51 THRU HI=3)
```

The keyword ELSE is an additional convenience in recoding whenever you want to recode a residual group of values for a variable into a single catchall category. The keyword ELSE is entered as follows: (ELSE=value.) This specification will cause any values which have not previously been reassigned to be set equal to the value in the (ELSE=value) expression. Because recoding assignment is done from left to right, it is *critical* that the ELSE recode expression be the *last specification* on the RECODE list. The following example illustrates how to use the keyword ELSE.

```
1                16
RECODE           RELIGION (LOWEST THRU 27=1)(30 THRU 34=2)(36 THRU 38=3)
                 (40 THRU 50,54=4)(ELSE=9)
VALUE LABELS     RELIGION (1) PRACTICING PROTS (2) PRACTICING CATHOLICS
                 (3) PRACTICING JEWS (4) PRACTICING OTHER (9) ALL NON-PRACTICING
```

In this example we have a hypothetical detailed code of religious affiliation and practice. The RECODE above assigns all types of practicing Protestants to code 1, all practicing Catholics to code 2, practicing Jews to 3, and the practicing affiliates of all other religions to 4. Finally, through the use of the ELSE keyword, all nonpracticing respondents, irrespective of religious affiliation, are assigned to code 9.

6.1.3 DIFFERENTIATING BETWEEN BLANKS AND ZEROS: THE KEYWORD BLANK

Many raw-input-data files are prepared with blank entries when information has not been ascertained. This is particularly true when no missing value codes are specified at the coding stage. Blanks are treated by SPSS as zeros and normally can be referred to as zeros on all value lists in SPSS control cards—including the RECODE card. However, your file may contain one or more variables that have *both* blank and zero as legitimate codes. If you wish to distinguish between these two, you can recode the blanks with the (BLANK=value) specification on the RECODE card. This will cause all blanks in the variable or variables being recoded to be set equal to the value in the (BLANK=value) expression.

You must place the (BLANK=value) specification on the RECODE list before any implicit or explicit recoding of the value zero. If SPSS encounters a recoding of the value zero first, all blanks will be recoded to the same code to which the zeros have been recoded.

The following example illustrates the correct use of the keyword BLANK.

```
1                16
RECODE           INCOME(BLANK=9)(0 THRU 5000=1)(5000 THRU 10000=2)
                 (10000 THRU HI=3)
VALUE LABELS     INCOME(1)LOW (2)MEDIUM (3)HIGH (9)NOT ASCERTAINED
```

In this example, all respondents for whom income information was not reported are assigned the code 9 (not ascertained), while all respondents who actually have zero income are assigned the code 1 (low).

Say that the RECODE card had read this way:

```
1                16
RECODE           INCOME (0 THRU 5000=1)(5000 THRU 10000=2)
                 (10000 THRU HI=3)(BLANK=9)
```

In this case, the respondents for whom the INCOME value was blank would nevertheless be assigned the code 1 (low income), because the recode specification for the value of zero (0) appears before the (BLANK=9) specification.

To avoid confusion and wasted time in recoding, you are encouraged *not* to use the blank as a legitimate category when coding and punching your data.

6.1.4 PLACEMENT OF THE RECODE CARD

Whenever you process information from a raw-input-data file, you must place the RECODE cards after the initial data-definition cards and before the first set of task-definition cards. ("Task-definition" cards convey commands for processing of the data, such as statistical analyses. See Chap. 7 for further details.) When processing from a system file, be sure the RECODE cards follow the GET FILE card and appear before the first set of task-definition cards. All VAR LABELS and MISSING VALUES cards applying to variables altered by RECODE cards would logically come after the RECODEs (and before the first task-definition cards), but you may place them before the RECODEs if you wish.

RECODE instructions are executed in the order of their appearance among the SPSS commands. In addition, their effects are cumulative. After a variable has been recoded, it may be recoded again by a subsequent specification on the same RECODE card or by a later RECODE card. In either case, the second set of instructions operates on the *new* values generated by the first set of RECODE instructions. Any changes created by RECODE cards are in effect throughout that run. In this sense, the RECODE card is considered a "permanent" transformation. The new values are not preserved beyond the end of the run, however, unless a SAVE FILE instruction appears in the control-card deck to create a new or updated saved file.

Example 6.1 illustrates the control-card setup for an analysis of four variables from the Organizational Membership Study. Although this example is meant to use the same raw *data cards* as printed in Appendix A, this is a completely separate file-creation run from the one which created the ORGSTUDY file. Raw data files may be processed by SPSS as many times as you wish, and each time you may use different names, labels, and missing values for the variables if desired. Indeed, the education and age variables were named differently in Example 6.1 from the way they were named when the ORGSTUDY file was created.

```
1                  16
FILE NAME          EX61, EXAMPLE 6.1 BASED ON ORGSTUDY DATA
DATA LIST          FIXED/ 1 EDUC SEX RACE 33-35 AGEGROUP 28-29/
INPUT MEDIUM       CARD
N OF CASES         350
RECODE             AGEGROUP(LO THRU 29=1)(30 THRU 44=2)(45 THRU 59=3)(60
                      THRU 97=4)
RECODE             EDUC (2=1)(4=3)(6,7=5)/ RACE(3 THRU 8=2)
VALUE LABELS       AGEGROUP(1)UNDER 30 (2) 30-44 (3) 45-59 (4) 60+/
                   EDUC (1) 0-8 (3) 9-12 (5) BEYOND H.S./
                   RACE(1) WHITE (2) NON-WHITE/
                   SEX (1)MALE (2)FEMALE/
MISSING VALUES     RACE(0)/ AGE(98,99)/ EDUC (0,9)
FREQUENCIES        GENERAL = EDUC TO AGEGROUP
READ INPUT DATA
                        .                    .
                        .                    .
                        .                    .
       (DATA CARDS WOULD APPEAR HERE)
                        .                    .
                        .                    .
                        .                    .
FINISH
```

EXAMPLE 6.1

Notice that the RECODE cards come after the DATA LIST. This is necessary, because the variable names used in the RECODEs must be identified to SPSS before the program knows that they are legitimate. Two RECODE cards are used here, although these transformations could be specified just as well with one long RECODE or three short ones (one for each variable). The VALUE LABELS and MISSING VALUES appear next. If the VALUE LABELS and MISSING VALUES cards had been placed before the RECODEs, they would have been punched in the same way, because RECODE specifications do *not* alter specifications on VALUE LABELS and MISSING VALUES instructions. Finally, the FREQUENCIES card requests frequency counts on the four variables, the data are supplied, and a FINISH card completes the SPSS instructions (these last three cards are explained in later chapters). In this example the intermediate system file is not saved, because a SAVE FILE card is not included.

6.2 TEMPORARY RECODING: THE *RECODE CARD

The permanent RECODE instruction produces data modifications which remain in effect throughout the entire SPSS run regardless of the number of analyses being performed. You will sometimes find situations, however, where it is desirable to have the data modifications in effect only for a single statistical analysis. This is achieved with the *RECODE card, which is called a "temporary" recode instruction. Its effect disappears as soon as the following task is completed.

While a permanent RECODE card may appear only before the *first* set of task-definition cards, the *RECODE card may appear before *any* task cards. If both RECODE and *RECODE cards are used before the first task, the temporary *RECODEs must be placed *after* all of the permanent RECODEs. *RECODE cards may *not* be used with SPSSG, the "miniversion" of SPSS.

Example 6.2 illustrates the use of the *RECODE card. Here, the ORGSTUDY system file is being used as it was created by the data-definition cards given in Appendix A. Consequently, the variable names given at that time must be used now. The education and race variables are permanently recoded in the same way as was done in Example 6.1. Corresponding changes are then made to the value labels. Notice that no changes need be made to values that no longer exist (such as values 2, 4, 6, and 7 on EDRESPON), because those labels will no longer be accessed.

```
1               16
GET FILE        ORGSTUDY
RECODE          EDRESPON (2=1) (4=3)(6,7=5)
RECODE          RACE (3 THRU 8=2)
VALUE LABELS    EDRESPON (1) 0-8 (3) 9-12 (5) BEYOND H.S./
                RACE (2) NON-WHITE/
*RECODE         AGE(LO THRU 29=1)(30 THRU 44=2)(45 THRU 59=3)(60 THRU
                97 =4)/  EDRESPON (3 = 1)
FREQUENCIES     GENERAL=EDRESPON, RACE, AGE, SEX
*RECODE         AGE(LO THRU 29=2)(30 THRU 39=3)(40 THRU 49=4)(50 THRU
                59=5)(60 THRU 69=6)(70 THRU 79=7)(80 THRU 89=8)
                (90 THRU 97=9)
FREQUENCIES     GENERAL=AGE
SAVE FILE       ORGDATA2, ORGSTUDY DATA WITH EDRESPON AND RACE RECODED
FINISH
```

EXAMPLE 6.2

A temporary recode comes next; it groups the age variable and makes a further, but temporary, change to EDRESPON. (A side effect of the latter change is that the label for value 1 on EDRESPON is temporarily inappropriate. Nothing can be done about this, because labels cannot be changed temporarily.) The first *RECODE is followed by a FREQUENCIES card requesting frequency counts for EDRESPON, RACE, AGE, and SEX. The case distributions on these variables will reflect the permanent and temporary recodes, but the changes induced by the *RECODE will be nullified as soon as this statistical task is finished.

A second *RECODE collapses the age variable into a new set of categories. The original coding scheme (exact years) is used on the left side of the equals sign, because the changes made by the first temporary recode are no longer in effect at this point. A second FREQUENCIES card requests a frequency distribution on the second recoding of the age variable.

Finally, these cards are followed by SAVE FILE and FINISH cards. The SAVE FILE causes a new version of the system file to be saved with a file name of ORG-DATA2. The new file will contain the permanently recoded versions of EDRESPON and RACE and the new VALUE LABELS. None of the temporary recodes will be saved because none appeared immediately prior to the SAVE FILE card.

6.3 TRANSFORM CARD

When using SPSS-mini, an additional card is required to achieve data modifications. This is the TRANSFORM card. It merely contains the control word TRANSFORM in the control field without any further specifications. Thus, it would appear as follows:

In the regular and maxiversions of SPSS, data modifications are performed at the same time that the data are processed by the next task. Space limitations prohibit that approach in SPSS-mini. Instead, permanent data modifications are made as a separate task. This is the function of the TRANSFORM card, and, if it is needed, it must be the first task. See Chap. 7 for further information about task-definition cards. In particular, note that a READ INPUT DATA card and the raw input data, if on cards, must immediately follow the TRANSFORM card when the run is processing raw data.

Example 6.3 illustrates the use of the TRANSFORM card. Two variables from the American Small Communities Study, MEDSCH and MEDFINC, are collapsed into three categories—low, medium, and high. The actual task of performing the recodes is initiated by the TRANSFORM card. The second task is to crosstabulate the new values of MEDSCH and MEDFINC, which will produce a 3 × 3 table.

```
1                16
GET FILE         COMSTUDY
RECODE           MEDSCH (LOWEST THRU 9.5=1) (9.5 THRU 12.0=2)(12.0 THRU
                    HIGHEST=3)/
                 MEDFINC (LOWEST THRU 4500=1)(4500 THRU 8000=2)(8000
                    THRU HIGHEST=3)
VALUE LABELS     MEDSCH MEDFINC (1)LOW (2)MEDIUM(3)HIGH
TRANSFORM
CROSSTABS        TABLES = MEDSCH BY MEDFINC
FINISH
```

EXAMPLE 6.3

6.4 OTHER DATA-MODIFICATION INSTRUCTIONS

Several other data-modification instructions also exist in SPSS, such as the COMPUTE, IF, and COUNT commands. These are not discussed in detail in the primer, but it is worth mentioning briefly what they do. You can find full details in the SPSS manual.

The COMPUTE instruction causes a variable to be assigned a value according to some mathematical formula. The variable receiving the value may be an existing variable you wish changed. Alternatively, you can create an entirely new variable with the COMPUTE instruction. A very wide range of mathematical operations can be used to create the expression which determines the new value. These operations include simple arithmetic, such as addition, subtraction, multiplication, and division, as well as more complex operations, such as square roots and logarithms. The following are some examples.

```
1                16
COMPUTE          X = X + 5
COMPUTE          ZAGE = (AGE - 47.39) / 10.62
COMPUTE          YHAT = 7.23 + (6.77 * MEDSCH) + (1.29 * MEDFINC)
```

The first example shows the old value of variable X being increased by 5 for each case. A new variable is being created in the second example. In this instance, the mean value of the variable AGE is being subtracted from each individual's age and the result is divided by the standard deviation to yield a z-score (the mean and standard deviation had been previously computed). The third example illustrates another common situation where you might wish to create a new variable. This situation is the computation of predicted values from a regression equation involving the variables MEDSCH and MEDFINC.

While the COMPUTE instruction performs the specified calculations for *every* case in your file, the IF instruction allows you to select only certain cases on which computations are to be performed. The selection is based on a logical condition. For instance, if you wish to add $2,000 to the income reported by elderly people in your survey, you might do this as follows:

```
1              16
IF            (AGE GE 65)   INCOME = INCOME + 2000
```

The portion in parentheses is the logical expression, which says, "Perform the computation for cases where AGE is greater than or equal to 65." The specified computation follows and has the same form as the COMPUTE specification. The logical conditions can be much more complicated than shown here and may involve comparisons between variables, comparisons between arithmetic expressions, and multiple conditions.

The COUNT instruction provides a means for creating an index based on the frequency with which certain values occur in a given list of variables. A simple example can be taken from the ORGSTUDY data set. If the variable NMEM did not already exist, we could create it as follows:

```
1              16
COUNT         NMEM = FRATMEM TO OTHMEM (1)
```

This statement says that, for each case, go through the variables included in the list from FRATMEM to OTHMEM and count up how many times the value 1 occurs and assign this result to the variable NMEM.

This summary of the COMPUTE, IF, and COUNT instructions was meant to give you an idea of the range of data modifications you may perform with SPSS. If you need any of these commands, the SPSS manual will provide you with detailed instructions.

7

TASK CARDS, RUN CARDS, AND THE ORDER OF CONTROL CARDS

Once you have prepared the data-definition and data-modification cards, if any, you will be ready to request the performance of various tasks. A *task* is an SPSS activity which processes or uses the data in some fashion. Most tasks involve the statistical analysis of the data, such as the preparation of frequency counts or crosstabulations. Other tasks process the data in other ways, as is the case with the SAVE FILE and TRANSFORM instructions. SPSS control cards which initiate data processing or analysis activities other than defining a file or specifying transformations are called *task-definition cards*.

The general nature and use of these cards are the main subject of this chapter. This chapter also explains two *run cards*, which are control cards that supply SPSS with supplementary information useful in executing or documenting your run. The proper placement and sequencing of data-definition, transformation, task-definition, and run cards conclude the chapter.

7.1 TASK-DEFINITION CARDS

Whereas the data-definition cards define the structure and contents of the data, the *task-definition cards* activate, define, and control the calculations to be performed on the data. While data-definition cards need not be changed from one computer run to another, you will be constantly preparing new task-definition cards as you proceed through each step of the data analysis.

Every task begins with a *procedure card*, which identifies the task to be performed and which provides detailed specifications necessary for the task. Statistical procedure cards may be followed by an OPTIONS card and/or a STATISTICS card if special options or additional statistics are desired. A READ INPUT DATA card is also needed with the first task when raw data are being processed. A procedure card plus any of the other three task cards (OPTIONS, STATISTICS, or READ INPUT DATA), if needed, are considered a single task. Each task reads the data file at least once and produces appropriate output. SPSS allows you to include an unlimited number of tasks in one run, with each being performed in the sequence in which it appears in the control-card deck.

7.1.1 PROCEDURE CARDS

The individual procedures which actually perform the calculations are subprograms of the SPSS system. A *subprogram* is a specific set of prestored program instructions which are designed to perform a particular task. You use *procedure cards* to select and activate the subprograms you wish to use. Each subprogram has a corresponding procedure card which begins with one or more special control words. The crosstabulation subprogram, for example, is activated by a procedure card having the control word CROSSTABS; a procedure card containing the control word T-TEST invokes the subprogram for computing *t*-tests; and so forth. The specification field contains the names of variables to be used in the calculations, as well as other information required to successfully complete the desired computations.

When SPSS encounters one of your procedure cards, it activates the desired subprogram. The subprogram then interprets the specification field, checks for OPTIONS and STATISTICS cards, and (if you made no errors) processes the data. The following procedure card would, for example, cause the crosstabulation subprogram to be executed and two joint frequency distribution tables to be generated—one for the variables RACE and INCOME and another for SEX and IQ. (This assumes, of course, that a file containing these variables has been properly defined.)

```
1              16
CROSSTABS      TABLES = RACE BY INCOME/ SEX BY IQ
```

Although all the procedure cards have a similar format, each of the subprograms is activated by a unique set of control words. In addition, the variable names and other specifications are entered onto the individual procedure cards under different notations, depending on the nature of the calculations performed. Following chapters will present detailed instructions on how to prepare a few of the more basic and important control cards. The SPSS manual, of course, contains explanations for all procedure cards.

7.1.2 OPTIONS CARD

The OPTIONS card provides SPSS with further information to be used in controlling a calculation that has been activated by a procedure card. The OPTIONS card enables you to choose among available subprogram options so that the output is tailored to your needs. For example, each of the subprograms contains several optional methods for processing missing data, and you can choose among these by means of the OPTIONS card. The OPTIONS card also allows you to select features which are specific to a particular subprogram. For example, the OPTIONS card which is used in conjuction with the CROSSTABS subprogram enables you to have your tables percentaged by columns, by rows, or in both directions. Every subprogram has a set of default options which are the processing features normally available. If you do not request a special option through the OPTIONS card, some other action will be taken by default. When all the default options are desired, you can skip preparation of the OPTIONS card.

The OPTIONS card contains the control word OPTIONS followed by a specification field which consists of a list of integer numbers that indicate the options desired within a given subprogram. Each option is identified and selected by a specific number. However, the options available, as well as their corresponding numbers, vary from one subprogram to the next. For this reason, the specific options available and their corresponding numbers are presented in the individual subprogram descriptions. The general format of the OPTIONS card is

An example OPTIONS card might appear as follows, where each of the numbers on the OPTIONS card activates one of the available subprogram options:

1	16
OPTIONS	1,2,5,7

If only one option is being requested, the control word OPTIONS must still include the final "S."

The OPTIONS card, and the STATISTICS card described below, are unlike most of the other SPSS control cards in that they must be completed on one physical card. The specifications *may not* be continued in columns 16 to 80 of a subsequent card. The OPTIONS card directly follows the procedure card to which it applies, although it may either precede or follow the accompanying STATISTICS card. The options selected are in effect only for the immediately prior procedure card.

7.1.3 STATISTICS CARD

The STATISTICS card is similar in structure and function to the OPTIONS card. This card enables you to select among a number of available statistics to accompany the calculations and to be reported on the output. For example, the subprogram CONDESCRIPTIVE (Descriptive Statistics for Continuous Data) allows you to have any or all the following statistics computed for the variables in the file: mean, standard deviation, standard error, variance, skewness, kurtosis, minimum, maximum, and range. Each of these statistics has an assigned number, and you may have the desired statistics computed by specifying the appropriate numbers. You may have *all* the available statistics for a given subprogram reported by following the control word STATISTICS with the keyword ALL instead of the number list. Of course, the statistics available vary from subprogram to subprogram. Detailed descriptions of available statistics are given in the individual subprogram sections. When *no* additional statistics are desired, you may omit the STATISTICS card.

The general format of the STATISTICS card is

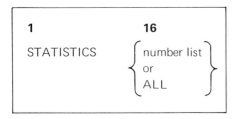

A sample STATISTICS card might appear as follows:

1	16
STATISTICS	2,4,5,7,9

The STATISTICS card directly follows the procedure card to which it applies but may be placed either before or after the accompanying OPTIONS card if one is used. As with the OPTIONS card, selected statistics are in effect only for the immediately prior procedure card.

7.1.4 READ INPUT DATA CARD

The READ INPUT DATA card instructs SPSS to begin reading the raw-input-data file. This card directly follows the OPTIONS and STATISTICS cards of the *first* group of task-definition cards. *When you are entering your data from cards, the data cards must immediately follow the READ INPUT DATA card.* This instruction contains the control words READ INPUT DATA in columns 1 to 15 and has no specification field. The READ INPUT DATA card is used whenever you are entering data from a raw-input-data file, whether these data are on cards, tape, disk, or any other medium. *This card is not used when processing from an SPSS system file alone* (i.e., when using the GET FILE command).

Example 6.1 from the previous chapter gives an illustration of how the READ INPUT DATA card is used. The first 12 control cards are data-definition and transformation instructions. The first (and only) task begins with the FREQUENCIES procedure card. Neither OPTIONS nor STATISTICS cards are desired here, so the next instruction is the READ INPUT DATA card followed by the actual raw data cards.

7.2 RUN CARDS

Run cards perform several auxiliary functions. Only two are of interest to the beginning SPSS user. You can find descriptions of the others in the larger manual.

7.2.1 RUN NAME CARD

The RUN NAME card allows you to supply a label to SPSS, which is then printed at the top of each page of output generated by the run. This is a convenient means for briefly identifying the purpose of the current SPSS run. The label may be up to 64 characters in length and may contain any of the valid characters allowed on your computer. The RUN NAME card may not be continued onto a second physical card. The card has the following format:

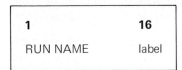

1	16
RUN NAME	label

An example RUN NAME card might be:

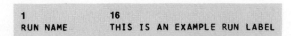

```
1               16
RUN NAME        THIS IS AN EXAMPLE RUN LABEL
```

The RUN NAME card is optional. If it is not used, blanks will appear in its place at the top of each page of printout. The RUN NAME card is normally the very first card in the control-card deck.

7.2.2 FINISH CARD

The FINISH card terminates processing for the current run and switches control from the SPSS system back to your computer's monitoring system. A FINISH card is always required, and it must be the last card in the control-card deck. Its format is as follows:

When SPSS encounters the FINISH card, it prints the following termination message:

NORMAL END OF JOB

XX CONTROL CARDS WERE PROCESSED

YY ERRORS WERE DETECTED

This message signifies normal SPSS termination, where XX is the total number of control cards processed by the system and YY is the number of control-card errors detected.

Whenever a run terminates without this message, it is a good indication that some problem was encountered which SPSS could not handle. For example, you might have given the computer the wrong definition of an SPSS input or output file, or you may have exceeded the specified time limit, the number of lines of output, or the available disk or core space. When your job does not end normally, check your printed output for error messages from the computer's operating system.

7.3 SUMMARY OF CONTROL-CARD ORDER AND DECK SETUP

All the basic control-cards necessary for beginners, except statistical procedure cards, have now been presented. Because proper placement of these cards in a control-card deck is essential to a successful run, we will review the placement rules here. Additional rules pertaining to control cards not discussed in the primer are given in the SPSS manual.

Because the control cards necessary for processing raw data differ significantly from those used with an existing system file, these two situations will be discussed separately.

7.3.1 CONTROL-CARD ORDER FOR PROCESSING RAW INPUT DATA

An initial file-generating run enables you not only to obtain the first set of desired calculations but also to save the file at the conclusion of the run. When a file is retained as an SPSS system file, the variable names, and their formats, as well as all the information entered on the data-definition cards, are permanently stored with the data. You need not save the system file. If you do, you will need the SAVE FILE instruction (Sec. 5.9.1). Either way, the general order of the cards is identical.

Table 7.1 summarizes the status of each control card and its precedence. *Precedence* means the relative position to be taken by the control card. Cards with lower precedence numbers come before those with higher numbers. Thus, the RUN NAME card must be first (if it is used), followed by FILE NAME, DATA LIST, INPUT MEDIUM, etc., in that order. Cards with the same precedence numbers may be intermixed among themselves as long as the group is kept in its precedence position. For instance, MISSING VALUES, VAR LABELS, VALUE LABELS, and RECODE may come in any order (if they are used at all), but all of them must come after the N OF CASES card and before the first set of task-definition cards. Task-definition cards all have a precedence level of 7, but within a single task the order is given by the letter following the number 7.

TABLE 7.1   Control-Card Order for Running with Raw-Input-Data Files†

Card status	Control field	Remarks	Precedence	
Optional	RUN NAME		1	
Conditional	FILE NAME	Required if an SPSS system file is to be saved, unless file name is given on SAVE FILE card.	2	
Required	DATA LIST		3	
Required	INPUT MEDIUM		4	Data-definition cards
Required	N OF CASES		5	
Optional	MISSING VALUES		6	
Optional	VAR LABELS		6	
Optional	VALUE LABELS		6	
Optional	RECODE		6	Data-modification cards
Conditional	TRANSFORM	Required in SPSS-mini when data transformations are requested. Must be followed by READ INPUT DATA. Not used in regular version of SPSS.	7B	
Optional	✳RECODE	Not allowed in SPSS-mini.	7A	
Required	procedure card	Any one procedure card.	7B	First task
Optional	OPTIONS		7C	
Optional	STATISTICS		7C	
Required	READ INPUT DATA		7D	
Optional	data cards	Required when raw input data are on cards. Placed immediately after READ INPUT DATA.		
Optional	✳RECODE	Not allowed in SPSS-mini.	7A	
Required	procedure card	Any one procedure card.	7B	Subsequent tasks if any
Optional	OPTIONS		7C	
Optional	STATISTICS			
Optional	SAVE FILE	Required to permanently save system file.	8	
Required	FINISH	Last card.	9	

†This table applies only to cards described in this primer. The use of other cards described in the SPSS manual may change the status and precedence of some of these cards.

Notice that the *first* task must include a READ INPUT DATA card, followed by the actual data cards (if the data cases are on cards). Subsequent tasks do not need this, because the raw input data are converted into an intermediate system file during the processing of the first task. This intermediate system file, which includes the results of any permanent transformations, is automatically available for use by all subsequent tasks. There is no limit to the number of subsequent tasks. Of course, you will not need any additional tasks if the first task produces all the statistics you desire.

The leftmost column of Table 7.1 describes the status of each card. "Required" cards are, of course, required. "Optional" cards are used at your discretion to achieve a desired effect. "Conditional" cards are needed only under certain conditions as noted in the remarks.

Example 7.1 illustrates a run using a raw-input-data file on cards. This example is meant to use the *raw* data from the Organizational Membership Study reported in Appendix A. Because the full set of data cards is so voluminous, they have not been reproduced here.

```
1              16
RUN NAME       FREQUENCY COUNTS ON SELECTED VARIABLES
DATA LIST      FIXED/ 1 RELIGION 27, INCOME 30-31, EDUC 33
INPUT MEDIUM   CARD
N OF CASES     350
MISSING VALUES RELIGION(0)/ INCOME(88,99)/ EDUC(9,0)/
FREQUENCIES    GENERAL = ALL
STATISTICS     3, 4
READ INPUT DATA
     .              .              .
     .              .              .
     .              .              .
(ALL 350 DATA CARDS FROM "ORGSTUDY" WOULD GO HERE)
     .              .              .
     .              .              .
     .              .              .
FINISH
```

EXAMPLE 7.1

In this example, the DATA LIST command is instructing SPSS to read only three variables—the ones dealing with religion, income, and the respondent's education. Notice that the variable names assigned here differ from those used when creating the ORGSTUDY system file. We did this to illustrate that you may use names different from those assigned by someone else *when you are processing raw input data*. If you do this, you must use the new names throughout that job and whenever processing a system file created by that job.

Example 7.1 contains only one statistical procedure. This is the FREQUEN-CIES subprogram, which will produce one-way frequency counts for all three variables being processed in this job. The additional statistics 3 and 4, which are the mode and median, will also be calculated. (Details about the FREQUENCIES procedure card, and the other statistical procedure cards used in the following examples, will be given in subsequent chapters.) Because this is the first task in a job processing raw input data, the task cards (i.e., the FREQUENCIES and STATISTICS cards) are immediately followed by the READ INPUT DATA card and the actual raw data cards (not shown). The last card is, of course, the FINISH card.

As you have probably noticed, several optional commands were omitted from Example 7.1. Because we did not wish to save the system file created by this run, we left out the SAVE FILE command. This made the FILE NAME card optional, so we omitted it, too. While variable and value labels are highly desirable, we did not provide VAR LABELS and VALUE LABELS cards to illustrate that these are optional.

The printed output produced by Example 7.1 is shown in Fig. 7.1. SPSS lists the control cards in sequence until it reaches the first task. After the DATA LIST command, SPSS prints the names and locations of each variable specified. This is followed by a "format statement," which is an internal instruction used by the computer to read your data. Normally, you do not need to be concerned with the format statement unless errors occur in reading the data. After SPSS locates the first set of task-definition cards, it performs the task and prints out the requested tables. Once these have been printed, SPSS searches for the next task, performs it, and searches further until the FINISH card is encountered.

As you can see, SPSS also prints information about the amount of transformation space and work space used by your job. The sizes of these spaces limit the number of transformation operations performed and the quantity of tables produced per run. As a beginner, you do not need to be concerned about the sizes of these spaces. The SPSS manual explains how to change the allocation and discusses strategies for using these spaces efficiently.

Example 7.2 illustrates another SPSS job which processes raw input data. The data being used here are the hypothetical data from Table 5.2. To keep the example short, only three data cases are included. Because there are 4 cards per case, this comes to a total of 12 data cards. Nevertheless, the N OF CASES is only 3. Some of the vari-

```
STATISTICAL PACKAGE FOR THE SOCIAL SCIENCES SPSSH - VERSION 6.00                    05/28/75        PAGE    1

                SPACE ALLOCATION FOR THIS RUN..

                    TOTAL AMOUNT REQUESTED                          50000 BYTES

                    DEFAULT TRANSPACE ALLOCATION                     6248 BYTES

                        MAX NO OF TRANSFORMATIONS PERMITTED     62
                        MAX NO OF RECODE VALUES                248
                        MAX NO OF ARITHM.OR LOG.OPERATIONS     496

                    RESULTING WORKSPACE ALLOCATION                  43752 BYTES

                        RUN NAME        FREQUENCY COUNTS ON SELECTED VARIABLES
                        DATA LIST       FIXED/ 1 RELIGION 27, INCOME 30-31, EDUC 33

        THE DATA LIST PROVIDES FOR  3 VARIABLES AND  1 RECORDS ('CARDS') PER CASE. A MAXIMUM OF   33 COLUMNS ARE USED ON A RECORD.

        DUMP OF THE CONSTRUCTED FORMAT STATEMENT..
              (26X,F1.0,2X,F2.0,1X,F1.0)

                        INPUT MEDIUM    CARD
                        N OF CASES      350
                        MISSING VALUES  RELIGION(0)/ INCOME(88,99)/ EDUC(9,0)/
                        FREQUENCIES     GENERAL = ALL
                        STATISTICS      3, 4

        GIVEN SPACE ALLOWS FOR  4372 TOTAL VALUES AND   437 LABELED VALUES PER VARIABLE FOR 'FREQUENCIES'

                        READ INPUT DATA
```

```
FREQUENCY COUNTS ON SELECTED VARIABLES                                              05/28/75        PAGE    2

    FILE   NONAME   (CREATION DATE = 05/28/75)

    RELIGION

                                        RELATIVE  ADJUSTED    CUM
                            ABSOLUTE      FREQ      FREQ      FREQ
    CATEGORY LABEL      CODE   FREQ       (PCT)     (PCT)     (PCT)

                        1.     239        68.3      68.5      68.5

                        2.      81        23.1      23.2      91.7

                        3.       6         1.7       1.7      93.4

                        5.      19         5.4       5.4      98.9

                        6.       1         0.3       0.3      99.1

                        7.       1         0.3       0.3      99.4

                        9.       2         0.6       0.6     100.0

                        0.       1         0.3     MISSING   100.0
                              ------     ------    ------
                    TOTAL      350        100.0     100.0

    MEDIAN    1.230    MODE     1.000

    VALID CASES    349    MISSING CASES    1
```

```
FREQUENCY COUNTS ON SELECTED VARIABLES                                              05/28/75        PAGE    3

    FILE   NONAME   (CREATION DATE = 05/28/75)

    INCOME

                                        RELATIVE  ADJUSTED    CUM
                            ABSOLUTE      FREQ      FREQ      FREQ
    CATEGORY LABEL      CODE   FREQ       (PCT)     (PCT)     (PCT)

                        1.      20         5.7       5.9       5.9

                        2.      24         6.9       7.1      12.9

                        3.      32         9.1       9.4      22.4

                        4.      32         9.1       9.4      31.8

                        5.      18         5.1       5.3      37.1

                        6.      32         9.1       9.4      46.5

                        7.      34         9.7      10.0      56.5

                       11.      30         8.6       8.8      65.3

                       21.      27         7.7       7.9      73.2

                       31.      16         4.6       4.7      77.9

                       41.      46        13.1      13.5      91.5

                       51.      19         5.4       5.6      97.1

                       61.       4         1.1       1.2      98.2

                       71.       6         1.7       1.8     100.0

                       88.       5         1.4     MISSING   100.0

                       99.       5         1.4     MISSING   100.0
                              ------     ------    ------
                    TOTAL      350        100.0     100.0

    MEDIAN    6.853    MODE    41.000
    VALID CASES    340    MISSING CASES    10
```

FIGURE 7.1

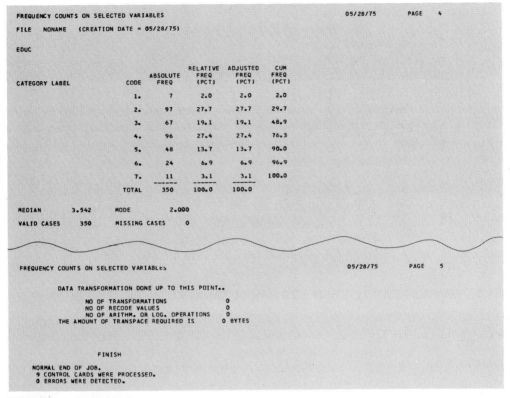

FIGURE 7.1   (continued)

```
1                    16
RUN NAME             INITIAL RUN ON HYPOTHETICAL DATA DESCRIBED IN TABLE 5.2
FILE NAME            ALLERGY, PHYSICAL CONDITIONS RELATED TO ALLERGIES
DATA LIST            FIXED(4)/ 1 EYECOLOR BALDNESS ANEMIA 26-28/ 2 SCORE1, SCORE2,
                     SCORE3, SCORE4 5-16 (2), HAYFEVER 57, ALGYCATS 63,
                     ALGYDOGS 64/ 4 SCALE15, SCALE16, SCALE17 30-35,
                     HRTBEAT 48-49, BLDPRESS 69-71
INPUT MEDIUM         CARD
N OF CASES           3
VAR LABELS           EYECOLOR, COLOR OF EYES/
                     BALDNESS, IS PATIENT BALD?/
                     SCORE2, AVERAGE SCORE ON S-J TEST/
                     SCALE16, REACTION TO POLLEN, CATS, & DOGS/
VALUE LABELS         EYECOLOR (1) BLUE (2) GRAY OR GREEN (3) BROWN (4) BLACK/
                     BALDNESS, ANEMIA, HAYFEVER TO ALGYCATS (1) YES (2) NO/
MISSING VALUES       EYECOLOR TO ANEMIA, HAYFEVER TO ALGYDOGS, SCALE16 (0,8,9)/
                     SCORE1, SCORE2(9.99)/ SCORE3, SCORE4, SCALE17, BLDPRESS(0)/
                     SCALE15(0,-1)/
RECODE               SCALE17(2,6,7=1)(5=3)
VALUE LABELS         SCALE17 (1) NO DANGER (3) DANGER (4) CRITICAL
CONDESCRIPTIVE       SCORE1 TO SCORE4, SCALE15, SCALE16, HRTBEAT, BLDPRESS
STATISTICS           ALL
READ INPUT DATA
00111009732533765201358634114548768095909117392927494537542048056489474296248052
00120842268953196450930323209025601595334764350803360699019025290937670715
00131280799970801573614764032366539895116877121717683366065747
00146606575717340727685036697361706581339885111992917065813398851798538
00213106010805455718240632103426148679907439234030973285269776020205165692686657
00226357332135053254704890553575482846828709834912562473096457890352964778
00239852017767149056860722109405586097093433505007399811805054
00248345299634062889808313746700711847540610687117781788685402008650758
00319959467348875176496991826089289378561368234783411365481176741746850950580477
00328012435635179270801545318223742111578253143855376374050998117740277214
00339149914523684792768646162835549475089923708920048800336945
00346991626803662522914836986872007662113990044005641809893205051422568
*RECODE               SCORE1, SCORE2 (9.989999 THRU 10 = 9.99)(0 THRU 5 = 1)(5 THRU
                      9.99=2)
FREQUENCIES          GENERAL = EYECOLOR TO SCORE2, HAYFEVER TO SCALE17
STATISTICS           1,5
OPTIONS              5,8
CROSSTABS            TABLES = HAYFEVER TO ALGYCATS BY EYECOLOR TO ANEMIA
OPTIONS              5
SCATTERGRAM          SCORE1, SCORE3 WITH BLDPRESS/ SCALE15 WITH SCALE16
SAVE FILE
FINISH
```

EXAMPLE 7.2

ables and values are labelled. One RECODE is performed (on SCALE17), followed by a VALUE LABELS card to describe the new values for SCALE17. The recode results, the missing value indicators, and all the labels will be saved in the system file. The first task is a CONDESCRIPTIVE procedure with a request for all supplementary statistics. The second task is a FREQUENCIES procedure preceded by a temporary recoding of SCORE1 and SCORE2. The temporary recoding results are in effect only for this FREQUENCIES procedure. Statistics 1 and 5 and options 5 and 8 are also requested as part of this task. Two more statistical tasks are requested—CROSSTABS and SCATTERGRAM procedures. Note that the OPTIONS and STATISTICS cards, when present, apply only to the immediately prior statistical procedure card. Any statistics or options requested for one procedure do *not* carry over to the next procedure. Consequently, no extra statistics will be produced for the CROSSTABS task. Neither additional statistics nor special processing options are requested for the SCATTERGRAM task. Finally, a SAVE FILE card is included so that the system file will be saved, and of course the required FINISH card comes last. No printed output from this job is shown here because the data are hypothetical.

7.3.2 CONTROL-CARD ORDER FOR PROCESSING FROM SPSS SYSTEM FILES

When an SPSS system file has been saved, it may be accessed at a later time for further processing. This is achieved through the GET FILE instruction. Because labels, missing value indicators, and permanent data transformations from the initial processing run are saved with the file, they should not be repeated when the system file is retrieved. Old labels and missing value indicators may be changed at this time, however. In addition, new data transformations, labels, and missing value indicators may be added. When this is done, the new version of the system file may be saved, if desired, through use of the SAVE FILE card. Of course, an unlimited number of statistical tasks may be performed. The READ INPUT DATA card is not needed, though, since no *raw* data are being processed. Table 7.2 summarizes the order in which you should place control cards when you are processing a system file.

Example 7.3 illustrates a run which is accessing an SPSS system file. The system file ALLERGY consists of the hypothetical data described in Table 5.2 and saved in Example 7.2. In Example 7.3, two variables are being recoded and value labels are provided to describe the new codes. This example assumes that SPSS-mini (SPSSG) is being used, so a TRANSFORM card is included. The TRANSFORM card actually defines the first processing task. The second task is the statistical procedure CROSSTABS. Notice that the READ INPUT DATA card is not used here, because the data are being retrieved from a system file.

```
1                16
RUN NAME         FURTHER ANALYSIS OF DATA FROM TABLE 5.2
GET FILE         ALLERGY
RECODE           SCALE15, SCALE16 (2=1)(3 THRU 6=2)(7 THRU HI=3)
VALUE LABELS     SCALE15, SCALE16 (1) LOW (2) MEDIUM (3) HIGH
TRANSFORM
CROSSTABS        TABLES=SCALE15 BY SCALE16
OPTIONS          5
STATISTICS       ALL
FINISH
```

EXAMPLE 7.3

A second example of processing from an SPSS system file is given in Example 7.4. This job uses data from the COMSTUDY system file. Because this file has already been created with the commands listed in Sec. A.1.2, the variable names must be spelled exactly as given in the Appendix. In this example, no transformations nor changes to the file-definition information were requested. Two statistical tasks are requested, and they will use the data as given in the system file. Notice that no extra statistics or special processing options were requested for the SCATTERGRAM

TABLE 7.2 Control-Care Order for Processing an SPSS System File†

Card status	Control field	Remarks	Precedence	
Optional	RUN NAME		1	
Required	GET FILE		2	
Conditional	FILE NAME	Required if a new varsion of the system file is to be saved with a new file name. May be omitted if new file name is given on SAVE FILE card.	3	New data-definition cards
Optional	MISSING VALUES		6	
Optional	VAR LABELS		6	
Optional	VALUE LABELS		6	
Optional	RECODE		6	Data-modification cards
Conditional	TRANSFORM	Required in SPSS-mini when data transformations are requested. Not used in regular version of SPSS.	7B	
Optional	✳RECODE	Not allowed in SPSS-mini.	7A	Task cards, repeat as needed
Required	*procedure card*	Any one procedure card.	7B	
Optional	OPTIONS		7C	
Optional	STATISTICS		7C	
Optional	SAVE FILE	Required to permanently save a new version of the system file.	8	
Required	FINISH	Last card.	9	

†This table applies only to cards described in this primer. The use of other cards described in the SPSS manual may change the status and precedence of some of these cards.

procedure. The OPTIONS card which follows the T-TEST card applies only to the T-TEST procedure.

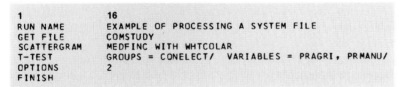

```
1                16
RUN NAME         EXAMPLE OF PROCESSING A SYSTEM FILE
GET FILE         COMSTUDY
SCATTERGRAM      MEDFINC WITH WHTCOLAR
T-TEST           GROUPS = CONELECT/  VARIABLES = PRAGRI, PRMANU/
OPTIONS          2
FINISH
```

EXAMPLE 7.4

8
DESCRIPTIVE STATISTICS AND ONE-WAY FREQUENCY DISTRIBUTIONS

SPSS contains two subprograms for computing statistics which summarize the pattern in which cases are distributed on single variables. These are CONDESCRIPTIVE and FREQUENCIES.

The name CONDESCRIPTIVE is short for CONtinuous DESCRIPTIVE statistics. This subprogram computes several summary measures of central tendency and variation. These measures are intended to describe variables measured on a continuous scale. A scale is continuous if a case can take any numerical value within the range of the scale, including fractional values. Examples would be a person's height and the percentage of the labor force employed in agriculture. A continuous scale must necessarily be an interval- or ratio-level measure. You may also find CONDESCRIPTIVE useful for any interval- or ratio-level variable even if it is not technically a continuous scale. This is especially true for variables with a great diversity of values represented among the cases, such as a person's age or a community's population.

The FREQUENCIES subprogram reports the frequency of occurrence of each unique value detected for a variable. The resulting table presents the raw count of cases for each value, the percentage of cases based on the total number of cases without a missing value on that variable, and cumulative percentages. Frequency counts are particularly useful for variables measured at the nominal or ordinal level and for interval-level variables consisting of a limited number of values. Some examples would be religion, political party affiliation, and the type of governmental structure of a community. One-way frequency distribution tables for such variables often serve as a computerized reference document for the file. Upon request, FREQUENCIES will also print a histogram (bar graph) and compute the summary measures available in CONDESCRIPTIVE.

8.1 SUMMARY OF SINGLE-VARIABLE DESCRIPTIVE STATISTICS

Normally, the first task you will undertake in any data analysis is to determine the pattern in which cases are distributed on each variable in your file. The characteristics you will usually check include measures of central tendency and variability—such as the mean, standard deviation, and range—and frequency counts of how often each value occurs in the particular data set.

These characteristics serve a number of functions. You will often find them useful just as they are. For example, the average percent population change, computed from the Communities Study data in Appendix A, might provide you with useful descriptive information about small communities. So might the proportions of communities with contested elections.

Distributional characteristics also frequently help you decide what analysis to perform next. For instance, some analytic techniques require variables that have a normal distribution, but others tolerate highly skewed variables.

Information about variable distributions may help you locate coding and keypunching errors. If, for instance, you find that the average percent population change is unusually high or low, you might suspect that a large number of coding or keypunching errors occurred or that you specified the wrong data-card columns for the variable. You would have even stronger evidence of errors if the frequency count showed the presence of values that should not exist. For instance, the occurrence of the value 6 on the CONELECT variable would signal an error, because category 6 has not been defined.

When a variable consists of only a few categories with many cases in each, you can easily grasp the pattern of distribution from the frequency table. In this situation, summary statistics help you to compare one pattern with another and allow you to briefly describe the general pattern. Summary statistics are all the more important, however, when the variable is a continuous scale or is comprised of many different values. This is so because the multiplicity of values makes it difficult for you to visualize and describe the complete pattern. Thus, both CONDESCRIPTIVE and FREQUEN-CIES compute several summary statistics which are briefly described in the remainder of this chapter. The mathematical formulas for computing these statistics are given in the SPSS manual, and further explanations on using the statistics can be found in most introductory statistics texts.

8.1.1 MINIMUM, MAXIMUM, AND RANGE

The *minimum* and *maximum*, of course, denote the smallest and largest values of a variable encountered among the cases. The *range* is the minimum subtracted from the maximum. These are suitable for use with variables measured at any level.

8.1.2 MODE

The *mode* is the value of the variable which occurs most often (not available in CONDESCRIPTIVE). For example, if you have six cases which have the values 6, 10, 10, 4, 4, 10 on VAR001, the mode of VAR001 is 10. If two or more values tie in having the "most" cases, then SPSS reports the lowest numerical value as the mode. The mode can be used with variables measured at any level.

8.1.3 MEDIAN

The *median* (not available in CONDESCRIPTIVE) is the numerical value of the middle case or the case lying exactly on the 50th percentile, once all the cases have been ordered from highest to lowest. For this statistic, SPSS assumes that the original measurement on the variable was continuous and interval-level but that the cases were subsequently grouped into categories. Consequently, SPSS computes the median by the method of interpolation (see the SPSS manual for details).

8.1.4 MEAN

The *mean* is the most common measure of central tendency for variables measured at the interval or ratio level. Often referred to as the "average," it is merely the sum of the individual values for each case divided by the number of cases.

8.1.5 VARIANCE

Variance is the measure of the dispersion of the data about the mean of an interval-level variable. This statistic is one way of measuring how closely the individual scores on the variable cluster around the mean. In its role as a measure of dispersion, variance plays an important part in many statistical tests and procedures. Indeed, one of the chief statistical goals of social research is to "explain" variance. This essentially means locating other variables which are related to the distance of a case from the mean on the given variable. Presumably, such variables can explain why the value for a case is not exactly equal to the mean.

8.1.6 STANDARD DEVIATION

The *standard deviation* is another measure of the dispersion about the mean of an interval- or ratio-level variable. Very simply, it is the square root of the variance. The advantage of the standard deviation is that is has a more intuitive interpretation, because it is based on the same measurement units as the original variable. If the variance of the ages in a sample of adults is 625, then we are really talking about 625 years-squared. The standard deviation, however, is 25 years, which has more intuitive meaning as the typical distance between any case and the mean.

8.1.7 STANDARD ERROR

If we were to draw an infinite number of equal-sized samples from a given population, the mean of each sample would be an estimate of the true population mean. But not all of these sample means would be identical. The pattern of these means would actually constitute a normal distribution and would have a standard deviation of its own. The standard deviation of *this* distribution is called the *standard error* of the mean. Thus, you can use the standard error to determine the potential degree of discrepancy between the sample mean and the (usually) unknown population mean. It requires interval-level measurement and is used in certain tests of statistical significance and for creating confidence intervals.

8.1.8 SKEWNESS

Skewness measures deviations from symmetry. Consequently, it indicates the degree to which a distribution of cases approximates a normal curve. The measure of skewness is sometimes called the "third moment." It takes a value of zero when the distribution is a completely symmetric, bell-shaped curve. A positive value indicates that the cases are clustered more to the left of the mean with most of the extreme values to the right. A negative value indicates clustering to the right. It is applicable for interval- and ratio-level variables.

8.1.9 KURTOSIS

Kurtosis is a measure of the relative peakedness or flatness of the curve defined by the distribution of cases. A normal distribution will have a kurtosis of zero. If the kurtosis is positive, then the distribution is more peaked (narrow) than would be true for a normal distribution, while a negative value means that it is flatter. Kurtosis is sometimes called the "fourth moment" and may be used only with interval-level data.

8.2 SUBPROGRAM CONDESCRIPTIVE: DESCRIPTIVE STATISTICS FOR CONTINUOUS VARIABLES

The subprogram to compute descriptive statistics for continuous interval-level data, CONDESCRIPTIVE, enables you to compute any one, a combination, or all of the following descriptive statistics for any or all of the variables in a file: mean, standard error, standard deviation, variance, kurtosis, skewness, range, minimum, and maximum. The specific statistics desired are selected by number on the STATISTICS card which follows the CONDESCRIPTIVE procedure card. All statistics computed by this subprogram assume that the variables for which they are computed are numerically coded and interval or ratio in scale.

8.2.1 CONDESCRIPTIVE PROCEDURE CARD

The procedure card for the CONDESCRIPTIVE subprogram begins with the control word CONDESCRIPTIVE starting in column 1. In the specification field you enter a list of variables for which you wish to have the descriptive statistics computed. You can enter the variable names by using the usual conventions for giving a variable list (see Secs. 5.5 and 6.1). If you want the statistics computed for *all* the variables in the file, you may simply enter the keyword ALL.

The general format of the CONDESCRIPTIVE procedure card is

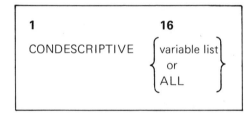

The following sample CONDESCRIPTIVE card would cause the desired statistics (selected on the STATISTICS card) to be computed for each of the variables listed on the card, as well as for all intervening variables implied between LIFE and READDIG. These variables are taken from the Communities Study file reported in Appendix A.

```
1            16
CONDESCRIPTIVE MEDSCH, MEDFINC, LIFE TO READDIG, POP60
```

Limitations on the number of variables to be processed at one time and the maximum number of elements to appear on the control card are given in the SPSS manual. These limitations are not likely to be exceeded by the beginning user. In the event that you do exceed them, a message will be printed and execution of your program will be stopped.

8.2.2 OPTIONS AVAILABLE FOR SUBPROGRAM CONDESCRIPTIVE

The CONDESCRIPTIVE procedure card may be followed by an OPTIONS card which informs the CONDESCRIPTIVE subprogram of the special processing options you desire. Any of the following options may be selected:

OPTION 1 Causes CONDESCRIPTIVE to include all cases in the computation of the statistics ragardless of whether some values were previously declared missing. If Option 1 is not exercised, the statistics computed for a given variable will be based only on cases which take values that have not been defined as missing.

OPTION 2   Suppresses the printing of extended variable labels which are normally reported on the output from this subprogram. This option slightly increases the processing speed of this subprogram.

OPTION 3   Causes *z*-scores to be computed and written onto an external medium for each case. See the SPSS manual for details.

OPTION 4   Causes a reference dictionary to be printed informing you of the page containing the descriptive statistics for any given variable. This reference dictionary appears after the last page of statistics.

The OPTIONS card may be deleted for subprogram CONDESCRIPTIVE. If it is not prepared, missing values will be excluded from the computations, the extended variable labels will be printed whenever present, no *z*-scores will be computed, and no reference index will be printed.

8.2.3 STATISTICS AVAILABLE WITH SUBPROGRAM CONDESCRIPTIVE

You may select among nine available statistics by placing the appropriate number(s) on the STATISTICS card. This card contains the control word STATIS-TICS, followed by a list of the numbers corresponding to the statistics desired. The available statistics and their corresponding numbers are:

1 Mean	**8** Skewness
2 Standard error	**9** Range
5 Standard deviation	**10** Minimum
6 Variance	**11** Maximum
7 Kurtosis	

When the number is placed in the specification field, that statistic will be computed for all variables named on the CONDESCRIPTIVE card. If all statistics are desired, the number list may be replaced by the keyword ALL. The following card will, therefore, cause all statistics to be computed and printed:

```
1              16
STATISTICS     ALL
```

If you should fail to enter a STATISTICS card, subprogram CONDESCRIPTIVE will calculate and print *all* the statistics listed above.

Note that there are no statistics corresponding to numbers 3 and 4. The purpose of this is to standardize the numbering of the statistics between procedures CON-DESCRIPTIVE and FREQUENCIES. We have left a gap for the median and the mode (Statistics 3 and 4), which are not available in subprogram CONDESCRIP-TIVE.

8.2.4 EXAMPLE OF THE USE OF SUBPROGRAM CONDESCRIPTIVE

Example 8.1 illustrates a typical setup for subprogram CONDESCRIPTIVE using the Communities Study system file described in Appendix A. Because a system

```
1              16
RUN NAME       CONDESCRIPTIVE OUTPUT CREATED BY EXAMPLE 8.1
GET FILE       COMSTUDY
CONDESCRIPTIVE PTGOHS TO PTMANU
STATISTICS     1,2,7,8,9
FINISH
```

EXAMPLE 8.1

file has already been created, all file-defining information and the data are retrieved with the use of the GET FILE card. The CONDESCRIPTIVE card causes statistics to be produced for the variables PTGOHS TO PTMANU. This implicitly requests analyses of the three consecutive variables PTGOHS, PTAGRI, and PTMANU. For each variable, Statistics 1, 2, 7, 8, and 9 are to be calculated—that is, the mean, standard error, kurtosis, skewness, and range. Full labelling, no z-scores, and no reference table will be produced, and only cases without a missing value on the respective variable will be used because no options were selected. The printed output tables are reproduced in Fig. 8.1.

```
CONDESCRIPTIVE OUTPUT CREATED BY EXAMPLE 8.1                              05/28/75      PAGE   2

FILE   COMSTUDY (CREATION DATE = 05/27/75)    STUDY OF AMERICAN SMALL COMMUNITIES


VARIABLE  PTGOHS      PERCENT TOTAL UNITS GOOD HOUSING

MEAN            75.161                STD ERROR        2.173              KURTOSIS       1.119
SKEWNESS        -0.965                RANGE           77.800

VALID OBSERVATIONS -      57                  MISSING OBSERVATIONS -        7

- - - - - - - - - - - - - - - - - - - - - - - - - - - - - - - - - - - - - - - - - - - - - - - -

VARIABLE  PTAGRI      PERCENT LABOR IN AGRICULTURE-FOREST-FISH

MEAN            12.087                STD ERROR        2.135              KURTOSIS       2.302
SKEWNESS         1.687                RANGE           71.900

VALID OBSERVATIONS -      61                  MISSING OBSERVATIONS -        3

- - - - - - - - - - - - - - - - - - - - - - - - - - - - - - - - - - - - - - - - - - - - - - - -

VARIABLE  PTMANU      PERCENT LABOR IN MANUAL OCCUPATIONS

MEAN            25.092                STD ERROR        1.947              KURTOSIS      -0.959
SKEWNESS         0.156                RANGE           57.800

VALID OBSERVATIONS -      63                  MISSING OBSERVATIONS -        1
```

FIGURE 8.1

8.3 SUBPROGRAM FREQUENCIES: ONE-WAY FREQUENCY DISTRIBUTIONS WITH DESCRIPTIVE STATISTICS

Subprogram FREQUENCIES computes and presents one-way frequency distribution tables and, if requested, a number of descriptive statistics.

Subprogram FREQUENCIES operates under two modes—GENERAL and INTEGER. The GENERAL mode produces frequency tables for all types of variables, while INTEGER mode operates only on variables whose values are all numeric integers. INTEGER mode operates significantly faster and can process more variables in a given amount of core storage space than GENERAL mode can. On the other hand, INTEGER mode requires you to enter the lowest and highest values of each variable. Because it is easier to use, we will describe only the GENERAL mode in this primer. See the SPSS manual for details on the use of INTEGER mode processing.

8.3.1 FREQUENCIES PROCEDURE CARD

The procedure card for the FREQUENCIES subprogram begins with the control word FREQUENCIES starting in column 1. Follow this in the specification field with one of the two keywords, GENERAL or INTEGER, depending on which operating mode you desire. At this point, the FREQUENCIES card would appear as follows:

1	16
FREQUENCIES	GENERAL=
	or
	INTEGER=

After the equals sign list the variables for which you want frequency tables and descriptive statistics. The format of the variable list differs between GENERAL and INTEGER modes. Only the GENERAL mode will be described here.

In GENERAL mode, you enter the variable list as you would the typical SPSS variable list, following the same conventions used in subprogram CONDESCRIPTIVE. If you wish frequency tables generated for all variables in your file, you may enter the keyword ALL instead of a variable list.

When operating subprogram FREQUENCIES under GENERAL mode, the format of the FREQUENCIES card is as follows:

```
1              16

FREQUENCIES    GENERAL = ⎧variable list⎫
                        ⎨  or         ⎬
                        ⎩ALL          ⎭
```

The following FREQUENCIES card instructs SPSS to produce frequency tables for a list of variables including INCOME, AGE, RACE, SEX, and ITEM1 to ITEM10.

```
1              16
FREQUENCIES    GENERAL = INCOME AGE RACE SEX ITEM1 TO ITEM10
```

Limitations on the number of variables to be processed at one time and the maximum number of elements to appear on the control card are given in the SPSS manual. These limitations are not likely to be exceeded by the beginning user. In the event that you do exceed them, a message will be printed and execution of your program will be stopped.

8.3.2 OPTIONS AVAILABLE FOR SUBPROGRAM FREQUENCIES

To request special processing options for subprogram FREQUENCIES, you enter the appropriate numbers on an OPTIONS card. The OPTIONS card, along with a STATISTICS card if one is needed, directly follows the FREQUENCIES procedure card. Several of the options described below refer to features which have not been discussed here. Please consult the SPSS manual for complete details on them. The available options are as follows:

OPTION 1 Causes the missing value indicators to be ignored; all values are considered valid when computing percentages for the tables, computing summary statistics, and printing histograms. If Option 1 is not specified, missing values are reported in the raw, relative, and adjusted columns of the frequency tables produced under the normal table format. Only the raw frequency of missing values is presented under the condensed table format. However, when Option 1 is not used, missing values are excluded from the calculation of adjusted and cumulative frequencies, and from all statistics.

OPTION 2 Deletes value labels from frequency distributions. This option may slightly increase the program's capacity. It is, however, irrelevant when the tables are printed in condensed format (Option 6).

OPTION 3 Causes all output from subprogram FREQUENCIES, including the page headings, to be printed in an $8\frac{1}{2} \times 11$ inch space on the left side of the output page. You may then reproduce and bind the output in ordinary notebooks.

OPTION 4 Causes all printed output to be written on a permanent-print file (either tape or disk) instead of on the line printer. This file may be printed later on special paper or to obtain multiple copies.

OPTION 5 Causes the frequency tables for *all* requested variables to be printed in condensed format. Condensed format allows up to 132 values to be printed per page, as opposed to 15 to 20 for the normal format. This is achieved by rearranging the page layout, by not printing value labels, not printing percentages with missing data included, and by rounding the percentages to the nearest whole number. See the SPSS manual for an example.

OPTION 6 Causes the frequency tables for all requested variables which will fill more than one page to be printed in condensed format, while the frequency tables for all other requested variables are printed in normal fashion.

OPTION 7 Deletes all frequency distribution tables and causes only the summary statistics requested on the STATISTICS card to be printed. The statistics for as many variables as possible will be printed on each page of output. While this option increases slightly the capacity of the program, its major function is to enable you to obtain CONDESCRIPTIVE-type output for discrete variables where the median and/or mode are desired statistics.

OPTION 8 Causes a histogram to be printed for each variable listed on the FREQUENCIES card. The histogram appears directly following the variable's frequency table and associated statistics, and is a graphic display of the relative frequencies of the variable's values.

OPTION 9 Causes a reference dictionary to be printed informing you about the output page number where the frequency tables and descriptive statistics for any given variable can be found. This reference dictionary appears on the page following the last page of frequency tables and descriptive statistics.

If no OPTIONS card is included in the deck setup, the following default options will be in force:

(*a*) Missing data will be excluded from all percentage figures in integer mode and from the adjusted and cumulative frequency distributions in general mode. In both modes, missing data will be excluded from the computation of all statistics.
(*b*) All variable and value labels that exist will be printed in the appropriate places.
(*c*) Frequency distribution tables and desired statistics will both be printed.
(*d*) The printed output will be sent to the printer and not to a permanent print file.
(*e*) Frequency tables will be printed in normal format, and page headings will extend across the entire page.
(*f*) No histograms will be produced.
(*g*) No reference dictionary will be produced.

8.3.3 STATISTICS AVAILABLE WITH SUBPROGRAM FREQUENCIES

To indicate the statistics you wish to obtain, you can do one of two things. You can place the keyword ALL in the specifications field of the STATISTICS card, in which case you will receive all available statistics. Or, you can select a subset of statistics by placing the appropriate reference number for each desired statistic in the specifications field. Here are the reference numbers of the statistics available to you:

1	Mean	**5**	Standard deviation	**9**	Range
2	Standard error	**6**	Variance	**10**	Minimum
3	Median	**7**	Kurtosis	**11**	Maximum
4	Mode	**8**	Skewness		

Unlike subprogram CONDESCRIPTIVE, failure to enter a STATISTICS card means that *no statistics will accompany the frequency tables.*

8.3.4 EXAMPLE OF THE USE OF SUBPROGRAM FREQUENCIES

Example 8.2 illustrates a typical control-card deck for using subprogram FREQUENCIES when the data already reside in a system file. In this example, the

```
1              16
RUN NAME       FREQUENCIES OUTPUT CREATED BY EXAMPLE 8.2
GET FILE       COMSTUDY
FREQUENCIES    GENERAL = GOVSELCT PARTISAN PARTROLE
STATISTICS     ALL
OPTIONS        8
FINISH
```

EXAMPLE 8.2

system file being accessed contains the Communities Study data described in Appendix A. The FREQUENCIES procedure card requests tabulations for the variables GOVSELCT, PARTISAN, and PARTROLE. All of the summary statistics have been specified, and the optional histograms have been requested.

Figure 8.2 shows the printout produced for the variable GOVSELCT. Notice that the frequency table contains:

1 The value labels wherever present
2 The raw, or absolute, frequencies associated with each value
3 The relative frequencies with missing values included in the percentages
4 Adjusted relative frequencies with missing values excluded from the percentage base
5 The cumulative adjusted frequencies based on the nonmissing values

```
FREQUENCIES OUTPUT CREATED BY EXAMPLE 8.2                          05/28/75      PAGE   2

FILE   COMSTUDY (CREATION DATE = 05/27/75)   STUDY OF AMERICAN SMALL COMMUNITIES

GOVSELCT   METHOD OF SELECTING HEAD OF GOVERNMENT

                                       RELATIVE   ADJUSTED     CUM
                             ABSOLUTE     FREQ       FREQ      FREQ
CATEGORY LABEL        CODE     FREQ      (PCT)      (PCT)     (PCT)

DIRECT ELECTION        1.       48       75.0       78.7      78.7

ELECT LOCAL BOARD      2.        7       10.9       11.5      90.2

APPOINTED BY HIGHER    3.        3        4.7        4.9      95.1

OTHER                  4.        3        4.7        4.9     100.0

NO LOCAL HEAD          8.        2        3.1     MISSING    100.0

NA                     9.        1        1.6     MISSING    100.0
                               ------    ------     ------
              TOTAL             64       100.0      100.0
```

FIGURE 8.2

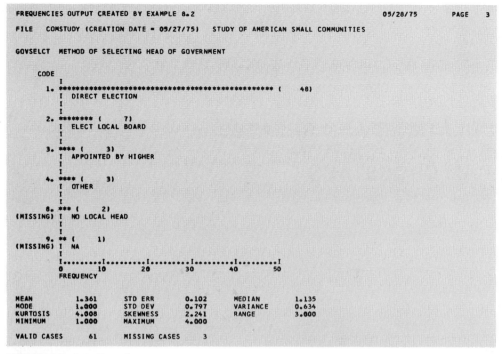

FIGURE 8.2 (continued)

9

CROSSTABULATIONS AND RELATED MEASURES OF ASSOCIATION: SUBPROGRAM CROSSTABS

After examining the distributional characteristics of each individual variable, you will most likely want to begin investigating relationships among two or more of your variables. Several types of statistical procedures are available for doing this. Crosstabulation analysis, regression analysis, and correlation analysis are a few of the many techniques available in SPSS. The type of analysis you choose will depend upon the characteristics of your variables and the research question you are attempting to answer. If you choose to perform a crosstabulation analysis, then you will need to use the CROSSTABS subprogram.

9.1 INTRODUCTION TO CROSSTABULATION

A *crosstabulation* (also referred to as a *contingency table*) is *a joint frequency distribution of cases as defined by the categories of two or more variables.* The display of the distribution of cases is the chief component of contingency table analysis. Indeed, this is the most commonly used method of analysis in the social sciences. Often, however, we compute additional summary statistics from the table. The chi-square statistic will tell us the likelihood that the variables are statistically independent. Several *measures of association,* such as the contingency coefficient, phi, tau, gamma, etc., are also available. They tell us the degree to which a case's value on one variable is related to its value on the other variable. In this section, we will first describe the basic nature of crosstabulations and then review the use of summary statistics.

9.1.1 CROSSTABULATION TABLES

We can best see the nature of crosstabulation tables by studying some typical examples of such an analysis. Consider a study which hypothesizes a relationship between hair and eye color—specifically, that the incidence of blue eyes among individuals with blond hair is considerably greater than the incidence of blue eyes among individuals with brown hair. If a survey collecting this information were taken, we could test the above hypothesis with the following type of 2 × 2 table:

Hair Color

	Blond	Brown
Blue		
Nonblue		

Eye Color

Let us further assume that the study examined 100 blond-haired and 200 brown-haired individuals and that the tabulation of the data indicated the following frequency distribution:

Hair Color

	Blond	Brown	
Blue	75	40	115
Nonblue	25	160	185
	100	200	

Eye Color

We can easily see that there are dramatic differences in the proportions of the blond-haired and brown-haired with blue eyes. Because, however, there are different total numbers of the blond-haired and the brown-haired, we more clearly see the exact difference when the proportions are displayed as percentages:

Hair Color

	Blond		Brown		
Blue	75%	(75)	20%	(40)	115
Nonblue	25%	(25)	80%	(160)	185
	100%	100	100%	200	

Eye Color

Obviously, there is a strong relationship between the color of hair and the color of eyes. But the results of a typical contingency table are often less dramatic than this, and the question usually emerges as to whether the differences in the percentages are statistically significant. Without attempting here to raise a question best answered in basic statistics books, there are a number of ways in which the percentages may be examined (provided the sample is more or less random) which can indicate whether discrepancies in percentages are due solely to sampling error or whether they reflect statistically significant relationships. (A number of tests of significance and association available in CROSSTABS are described briefly below.)

There are two logical extensions of this basic table: the addition of other variables as controls and the addition of categories within the variables. To demonstrate these logical extensions, let us shift to a less obvious and more interesting example. Consider

FIGURE 9.1

a study which is concerned with the relationship between race and income. Let us formulate two simple hypotheses for this study: (1) there is a relationship between race and income—i.e., that nonwhites have considerably less income than whites, and (2) while part of this relationship is due to the differential levels of educational attainment between nonwhites and whites, the basic relationship between race and income persists even after controlling for educational attainment. To test these hypotheses, we can examine tables computed from the ORGSTUDY data reported in Appendix A. Figure 9.1 gives the table for the income and race relationship. (The categories for each variable were combined into a more manageable number and relabelled.)

It is evident from Fig. 9.1 that there is a strong relationship between race and income. The proportion of whites in the higher-income categories is considerably greater than the proportion of nonwhites in the higher-income categories, and the opposite is true in the lower-income categories.

The second hypothesis, that this relationship persists even when controlling for levels of education, requires a three-dimensional table. Because printing surfaces are two-dimensional, three-dimensional tables are usually presented as a series of two-dimensional tables on separate computer printout pages. Values on the control variable (education, in our example) determine which cases are used in constructing the sub-tables. As you can see in Fig. 9.2, the first table includes only those cases with the value 1 on variable EDRESPON (after recoding, these are persons with less than a high school education). Similarly, the second table contains only respondents with the value 2 on EDRESPON (high school or more education, after recoding). We can now see that the same general pattern persists within each education group. This confirms our second hypothesis, that nonwhites tend to have lower incomes even after controlling for educational attainment.

Figure 9.2 illustrates the classical approach to "elaboration analysis." You begin by examining a bivariate table (as was done above for income and race), and you then successively enter control variables (in this instance, education) to see what role they play in the basic relationship. In the example above, we see that for each racial group, having more education is associated with having higher income. Nevertheless, the relationship between race and income remains strong even after controlling for education. If one were seriously interested in pursuing the hypothesis that lower income for nonwhites is a direct result of racial discrimination, other control variables should be entered both as a series of first-level controls (producing three-variable tables) and as combinations of the control variables. The usual attempt here is to find a control vari-

```
STATISTICAL PACKAGE FOR THE SOCIAL SCIENCES SPSSH - VERSION 6.00                    05/28/75        PAGE    3

FILE   ORGSTUDY (CREATION DATE = 05/27/75)   STUDY OF ORGANIZATIONAL MEMBERSHIP AND ACTIVITY

* * * * * * * * * * * * * * * * *   C R O S S T A B U L A T I O N   O F   * * * * * * * * * * * * * * * * * * *
     INCOME    FAMILY INCOME                                    BY RACE      RESPONDENT'S RACE
CONTROLLING FOR..
     EDRESPON  LAST YEAR OF SCHOOL COMPLETED                    VALUE =        1.  LESS THAN H.S.
* * * * * * * * * * * * * * * * * * * * * * * * * * * * * * * * * * * * * * * * * * * * *  PAGE  1 OF  1

                   RACE
          COUNT  I
          COL PCT IWHITE    NONWHITE    ROW
                  I                     TOTAL
                  I    1.I      2.I
INCOME    --------I--------I--------I
         1.      I     51 I     31 I     82
LESS THAN $4000  I   42.1 I   72.1 I   50.0
                 -I--------I--------I
         2.      I     44 I      9 I     53
$4000-$7999      I   36.4 I   20.9 I   32.3
                 -I--------I--------I
         3.      I     26 I      2 I     28
$8000-$14999     I   21.5 I    4.7 I   17.1
                 -I--------I--------I
         4.      I      0 I      1 I      1
$15000 AND OVER  I    0.0 I    2.3 I    0.6
                 -I--------I--------I
         COLUMN       121       43       164
         TOTAL       73.8     26.2     100.0

CHI SQUARE =    16.10907 WITH  3 DEGREES OF FREEDOM   SIGNIFICANCE = 0.0011
CRAMER'S V =   0.31341
CONTINGENCY COEFFICIENT =   0.29907
LAMBDA (ASYMMETRIC) = 0.0      WITH INCOME  DEPENDENT.          = 0.02326 WITH RACE     DEPENDENT.
LAMBDA (SYMMETRIC) = 0.00800
UNCERTAINTY COEFFICIENT (ASYMMETRIC) = 0.05038 WITH INCOME  DEPENDENT.          = 0.09147 WITH RACE     DEPENDENT.
UNCERTAINTY COEFFICIENT (SYMMETRIC) = 0.06498
KENDALL'S TAU B =   -0.24881 SIGNIFICANCE =  0.0004
KENDALL'S TAU C =   -0.24301 SIGNIFICANCE =  0.0004
GAMMA =   -0.51481
SOMERS'S D (ASYMMETRIC) = -0.31405 WITH INCOME  DEPENDENT.        = -0.19713 WITH RACE    DEPENDENT.
SOMERS'S D (SYMMETRIC) = -0.24222
ETA = 0.24030 WITH INCOME  DEPENDENT.          = 0.31342 WITH RACE    DEPENDENT.
```

```
STATISTICAL PACKAGE FOR THE SOCIAL SCIENCES SPSSH - VERSION 6.00                    05/28/75        PAGE    4

FILE   ORGSTUDY (CREATION DATE = 05/27/75)   STUDY OF ORGANIZATIONAL MEMBERSHIP AND ACTIVITY

* * * * * * * * * * * * * * * *   C R O S S T A B U L A T I O N   O F   * * * * * * * * * * * * * * * * * * *
     INCOME    FAMILY INCOME                                    BY RACE      RESPONDENT'S RACE
CONTROLLING FOR..
     EDRESPON  LAST YEAR OF SCHOOL COMPLETED                    VALUE =        2.  H.S. OR MORE
* * * * * * * * * * * * * * * * * * * * * * * * * * * * * * * * * * * * * * * * * * * * *  PAGE  1 OF  1

                   RACE
          COUNT  I
          COL PCT IWHITE    NONWHITE    ROW
                  I                     TOTAL
                  I    1.I      2.I
INCOME    --------I--------I--------I
         1.      I     15 I     11 I     26
LESS THAN $4000  I   10.2 I   37.9 I   14.8
                 -I--------I--------I
         2.      I     49 I     12 I     61
$4000-$7999      I   33.3 I   41.4 I   34.7
                 -I--------I--------I
         3.      I     56 I      5 I     61
$8000-$14999     I   38.1 I   17.2 I   34.7
                 -I--------I--------I
         4.      I     27 I      1 I     28
$15000 AND OVER  I   18.4 I    3.4 I   15.9
                 -I--------I--------I
         COLUMN       147       29       176
         TOTAL       83.5     16.5     100.0

CHI SQUARE =    19.48544 WITH  3 DEGREES OF FREEDOM   SIGNIFICANCE = 0.0002
CRAMER'S V =   0.33274
CONTINGENCY COEFFICIENT =   0.31572
LAMBDA (ASYMMETRIC) = 0.06087 WITH INCOME  DEPENDENT.          = 0.0      WITH RACE     DEPENDENT.
LAMBDA (SYMMETRIC) = 0.04861
UNCERTAINTY COEFFICIENT (ASYMMETRIC) = 0.03988 WITH INCOME  DEPENDENT.          = 0.11670 WITH RACE     DEPENDENT.
UNCERTAINTY COEFFICIENT (SYMMETRIC) = 0.05945
KENDALL'S TAU B =   -0.28618 SIGNIFICANCE =  0.0000
KENDALL'S TAU C =   -0.25349 SIGNIFICANCE =  0.0000
GAMMA =   -0.61286
SOMERS'S D (ASYMMETRIC) = -0.46047 WITH INCOME  DEPENDENT.        = -0.17786 WITH RACE    DEPENDENT.
SOMERS'S D (SYMMETRIC) = -0.25660
ETA = 0.31309 WITH INCOME  DEPENDENT.          = 0.33273 WITH RACE    DEPENDENT.

NUMBER OF MISSING OBSERVATIONS =     10
```

FIGURE 9.2

able or set of control variables which cause the income discrepancies between whites and nonwhites to disappear. If such control variables can be found, you would conclude that there is no direct effect of racial discrimination on income. Furthermore, these control variables would indicate why there are income differences between whites and nonwhites. On the other hand, if all reasonable control variables fail to nullify the relationship, you still will not have *proved* the hypothesis. But, at least, you will have failed in all attempts to falsify it. If the collection of control variables is comprehensive enough and you have wisely applied them, you will have some justification for claiming that racial discrimination has a direct effect on income levels "beyond a reasonable doubt."[1]

---

[1]For an excellent introduction to the logic of this type of contingency table elaboration analysis, see Morris Rosenberg, *The Logic of Survey Analysis,* Basic Books Inc., New York, 1968.

9.1.2 SUMMARY STATISTICS FOR CROSSTABULATIONS

Often it is desirable to summarize the relationship depicted in a crosstabulation table with a measure of association or a test of statistical significance.

A *measure of association* indicates how strongly two variables are related to each other. In essence, it measures the extent to which characteristics of one sort and characteristics of another sort occur together. For example, in our hypothetical study of hair and eye color we found that blond hair and blue eyes usually occur together, as do brown hair and dark eyes. A measure of association also indicates the extent that prior knowledge of a case's value on one variable better enables you to predict the case's value on the other variable. However, a measure of association tells us only how strongly the two variables are related in the cases that have been studied.

Social scientists usually study only a sample of all possible cases. Actually, we are not interested in the sampled cases per se, but rather we hope to infer that a relationship found in the sample actually exists in the population represented by the sample. A problem arises here—how are we to infer that the relationship actually does exist in the larger population? To return to our example, perhaps there is *no* universal relationship between hair and eye color and we have just been unlucky enough to draw a very unrepresentative sample. If we were to draw another sample of 300 people, perhaps we would find a very different relationship. It is here that tests of statistical significance come into play.

With the chi-square test of statistical significance we learn the probability that the observed joint distribution of cases would have happened by chance when no association exists between the two variables in the population. Actually, the chi-square statistic itself is not a probability, but it can be converted into a *probability figure* which we customarily call the *significance level*. SPSS does this conversion for you and prints the significance level along with the chi-square value.

Social scientists typically accept as statistically significant those relationships which have only a .05, .01, or .001 probability of occurring by chance. The specific level you use depends upon your personal preference and the degree of risk you are willing to take in making a wrong inference. A .05 significance level means that, if the same type of random sample were drawn from the population an infinite number of times, you would observe only 5 out of every 100 to have that strong or stronger a relationship when the variables are actually unrelated. If your table has a .05 significance level (or even something smaller, like .01), you know that the pattern was very unlikely to have occurred by chance. Although it could be one of those 5 out of 100, you are taking a very small risk in assuming that it is not.

The mere fact that a relationship is statistically significant does not mean that the degree of relationship is important in the context of your substantive research. The size of the sample greatly affects the significance level. Indeed, significance tests are mostly a measure of whether your sample is sufficiently large to be undisturbed by the chance selection of unrepresentative cases. In very large samples, weak relationships will prove to be statistically significant even though the relationship is too slight to be meaningful for your research.

The chi-square statistic tests only the general distribution in the table. It makes no assumptions about the level of measurement, and it does not report the strength of the association. Subprogram CROSSTABS, however, does offer several measures of association which you can use to determine how strong a relationship there is between the variables. Most measures of association also have tests for their statistical significance. In this instance, the significance level is the probability of securing a relationship that is strong or stronger in your sample when there is no relationship in the population.

Each of the available statistics is applicable in slightly different situations. SPSS computes whatever statistics you select; it is up to you to determine which are appropriate for the data.

The choice of a test of significance or measure of association depends in part upon the level at which the two variables employed in the crosstabulation are measured. The chi-square test of statistical significance and four measures of association (Cramer's V, the contingency coefficient, lambda, and the uncertainty coefficient) assume that both variables in the table were measured at the nominal level. You may apply these statistics to tables composed of variables measured at a higher level, but the statistics are calculated *as if* the variables were measured at only the nominal level. The computational formulas ignore any information regarding the order of or distances between categories. You must keep this fact in mind when interpreting these statistics.

At least ordinal-level measurement is required for both variables when the tau *b*, tau *c*, gamma, or Somers' *D* measures of association are being used. Although you can apply them when one or both variables are at a higher level, such as the interval or ratio level, the information about distances between categories is ignored. When both variables are at the interval or ratio level, the Pearson product-moment correlation (computed by PEARSON CORR and SCATTERGRAM) is the most appropriate measure of association. These statistics have no meaning and should not be used when one or both of the variables have been measured at the nominal level.

Finally, the eta statistic assumes that the independent variable is nominal-level and the dependent variable is interval-level.

You can find complete statistical treatments of these measures of association in most introductory applied statistics texts. Computing formulas, basic assumptions, and some further guidelines for applying and interpreting these statistics are given in the SPSS manual.

When you ask SPSS to compute any of these statistics, they are printed directly below the table to which they apply. When crosstabulation tables are produced for three or more variables, the statistics printed below each subtable are *conditional* statistics describing the observed relationship between the two variables in the table *when the control variables are at the level specified*. In addition, when gamma is requested for tables with three or more variables, the zero-order gamma and the *n*th-order gamma describing the overall relationship between the variables are printed below the final subtable.

9.2 CROSSTABS PROCEDURE CARD

Crosstabulations are produced in SPSS by the CROSSTABS subprogram. CROSSTABS, like FREQUENCIES, operates under two modes—integer and general. Integer mode is restricted to operating on variables which contain only integer values. Although it requires more card preparation, it consumes less core storage and computer time. General mode can operate on any type of variable—integer, fractional, or alphabetic. When the variables contain only integer values, both modes will produce identical tables. This primer describes only the use of general mode. See the SPSS manual for an explanation of the additional integer-mode specifications.

The CROSSTABS procedure card begins with the control word CROSSTABS beginning in column 1. You indicate the tables desired in the specification field beginning in column 16. The keyword TABLES is punched first, followed by an equals sign, and then the list of tables, using the general format given below:

```
1              16
CROSSTABS      TABLES= {variable name}  BY  {variable name}  [BY ... BY  {variable name}]
                      {     or        }       {     or       }          {     or        }
                      {variable list  }       {variable list }          {variable list  }
```

In the TABLES= list, specify the desired tables by means of variable names linked with the keyword BY. For example, a two-way table with the AGE variable defining the rows and the SEX variable defining the columns is requested as follows:

```
1              16
CROSSTABS      TABLES = AGE BY SEX
```

To request a three-way table, append another BY and follow it with the variable name defining the third dimension. You can include additional dimensions, up to 10, by adding additional variable names separated by the keyword BY.

Thus, the keyword BY indicates that an additional dimension, or level of control, is desired. This is illustrated by the following requests, which specify three-way, four-way, and five-way tables, respectively.

```
1              16
CROSSTABS      TABLES = AGE BY SEX BY RACE
CROSSTABS      TABLES = AGE BY SEX BY RACE BY INCOME
CROSSTABS      TABLES = AGE BY SEX BY RACE BY INCOME BY EDUCATN
```

In the first specification, a separate crosstabulation of AGE by SEX would be produced for each category of the RACE variable. If there are only two racial categories (white and nonwhite), two subtables will be produced. One will contain the results for the white respondents while the other will contain the results for the nonwhite respondents. The presence of a fourth dimension will result in an even finer subdivision of cases. If INCOME has been grouped into three categories (low, medium, and high), the second specification above would produce six tables. An age-by-sex crosstabulation would be generated for every race and income combination—i.e., low-income whites, low-income nonwhites, medium-income whites, medium-income nonwhites, high-income whites, high-income nonwhites. Additional dimensions create even finer subdivisions of the cases. The last specification above would produce an age-by-sex table for every possible combination of the race, income, and education categories.

It is very important to understand the sequential order of the variables surrounding the BY designation: the first variable mentioned always becomes the row variable and the second is always the column variable; and if three or more variables are involved in one set of tables, the third variable becomes the lowest-order control variable, and so forth, moving to the right. The tables are printed out in sequence where the value for the last variable named changes most slowly. This was illustrated in the previous paragraph when naming the six AGE BY SEX BY RACE BY INCOME tables.

The following examples illustrate how different tables can be requested by changing the order of the variables.

```
1              16
CROSSTABS      TABLES = RACE BY INCOME
CROSSTABS      TABLES = INCOME BY RACE
```

The first TABLES= list will produce a table where RACE is the row variable, while the second specifies INCOME as the row variable. The difference can be seen in the following diagram:

		Income	
Race	Low	Medium	High
White			
Nonwhite			

		Race	
Income	White	Nonwhite
Low		
Medium		
High		

You should be particularly careful in sequencing your variables, since this will affect the computation of row and column percentages. Similarly, control variables will not serve as controls unless they are listed after the second BY.

Multiple tables can be specified on a single TABLES= list by several conventions. First, you can specify a number of individual tables by placing a slash [/] between the table requests. The slashes in the following specification, for example, will cause one table to be computed for RACE BY INCOME, another for URB BY EDUCATN, and a third for SEX BY OCCUPATN.

```
1               16
CROSSTABS       TABLES = RACE BY INCOME/ URB BY EDUCATN/ SEX BY OCCUPATN
```

The order in which tables are requested is unimportant except that the tables will be printed in that order. You can enter up to 20 lists separated by slashes in a TABLES= list.

You can also request multiple tables by placing more than one variable name to the right or left of any BY. This is done with the typical SPSS variable list which can name single variables or a group of adjacent variables, as in the following example:

VARA, VARD, VARF TO VARJ BY VARN, VARP TO VARQ, VARZ

Such multiple lists will produce one table for each variable named or implied on the left side of the BY for every variable named or implied to the right of the BY. The first variable named to the left of the BY becomes the row variable and will be crosstabulated with each variable named or implied to the right of the keyword BY.

The following examples demonstrate in greater detail how multiple table requests may be constructed.

```
1               16
CROSSTABS       TABLES = RACE,SEX,INCOME BY EDUCATN,OCCUPATN
CROSSTABS       TABLES = RACE BY SEX TO INCOME
CROSSTABS       TABLES = RACE TO OCCUPATN BY EDUCATN
CROSSTABS       TABLES = RACE TO OCCUPATN BY INCOME TO EDUCATN
CROSSTABS       TABLES = RACE TO OCCUPATN BY INCOME TO EDUCATN BY CITY
```

In the first example, RACE will become the first row variable and will be crosstabulated first with EDUCATN and then with OCCUPATN. SEX will then become the row variable to be crosstabulated with EDUCATN and OCCUPATN. This will be repeated for INCOME, which is the last row variable. In the second example, RACE is the only row variable, and one table will be produced for each variable (in the file) from SEX to and including INCOME. If there are five variables between and including these variables, five tables would be produced with RACE by SEX being the first table and RACE by INCOME being the last. In the third example, RACE will again become the first row variable, while EDUCATN will always be the column variable, and RACE will be replaced in turn by all variables falling between it and OCCUPATN in the variable list. In the fourth example, RACE will become the first row variable, and one table will be produced for each variable between and inclusive of INCOME and EDUCATN, which will all be column variables. A similar set of tables will be produced for each row variable between RACE and OCCUPATN. In the last and most complex example, there will be one table for each value of CITY for every combination specified (i.e., each combination of RACE TO OCCUPATN BY INCOME TO EDUCATN). In effect, CITY becomes the control variable for the entire set of tables that were generated in the fourth example.

In the above examples each set of table requests was placed on a separate TABLES= list. This was done solely for the sake of clarity and is not generally recommended, because each occurrence of a CROSSTABS procedure card causes a separate reading of your data. You can avoid this by making multiple requests on the same procedure card. Multiple lists can be entered onto a single TABLES= list as long as each list is separated from the next by a slash [/]. All the usual rules concerning continuing SPSS control cards from one physical card to the next apply when you cannot fit your request on a single card. In addition, variable names may not be split between cards, and the keyword BY must be separated from the variable names by one or more common delimiters.

Limitations on the number of tables to be prepared at one time and the maximum number of elements to appear on the control card are given in the SPSS manual. These limitations are not likely to be exceeded by the beginning user making only a modest request. In the event that you do exceed the limits, a message will be printed and execution of your program will be stopped.

9.3 OPTIONS AVAILABLE FOR SUBPROGRAM CROSSTABS: THE OPTIONS CARD

The OPTIONS card provides you with several types of processing options for subprogram CROSSTABS. These options are selected by number in the usual fashion, as described in Sec. 7.1.2. The following is a list of the options available and their corresponding option numbers:

OPTION 1 Causes values declared as missing to be included in the tables *and* the statistical calculations. If not used, the default option assumes that values defined as missing on the MISSING VALUES card are to be excluded from the tables and the statistics. The number of missing cases for any given table will be reported, however.

OPTION 2 Causes the search for and printing of labels to be suppressed. Both variable labels and value labels are suppressed by this option. When Option 2 is not used, the default option is to search for and print labels whenever present.

Options 3 to 5 deal with the table percentages to be printed. When the options are not used, each table is percentaged by row, by column, and by the cell percent of the total.

OPTION 3 Causes row percentages to be deleted.

OPTION 4 Causes column percentages to be deleted.

OPTION 5 Causes total percentages to be deleted.

Options 6, 7, and 8 are available only when integer mode processing is being used. They are explained in the SPSS manual.

OPTION 9 This option causes an index to be printed which lists all tables produced by the CROSSTABS procedure and the page number where each table begins. The index is printed on the page following the last page of tables requested on the CROSSTABS procedure card. If this option is not used, no index will be printed.

The OPTIONS card directly follows either the CROSSTABS card or the STATISTICS card and controls the options on all tables requested for that task. If the OPTIONS card is deleted, the default options will all be in force. This means that missing values will be excluded from the tables; labels will be printed where present; all tables will be percentaged by row, by column, and by total; and no index will be printed.

9.4 STATISTICS AVAILABLE FOR SUBPROGRAM CROSSTABS: THE STATISTICS CARD

As with most SPSS subprograms, you may select additional statistics by means of the STATISTICS card. The STATISTICS card directly follows either the OPTIONS

TABLE 9.1 **Correspondence between Statistics and Numbers for Subprogram CROSSTABS**

1 Chi square†	**6** Kendall's tau *b*
2 Phi for 2 × 2; *Cramer's V* for larger tables	**7** Kendall's tau *c*
	8 Gamma
3 Contingency coefficient	**9** Somers' *D* symmetric and asymmetric
4 Lambda symmetric and asymmetric	**10** Eta
5 Uncertainty coefficient symmetric and asymmetric	

†For 2 × 2 tables, Fisher's exact test is applied when there are fewer than 21 cases. Yates' corrected chi-square is applied for all other 2 × 2 tables.

‡Conditional gammas are available in both integer and general modes, but partial gamma is available in integer mode only.

card or the CROSSTABS card. Table 9.1 indicates the statistics available and their corresponding statistic numbers. If the keyword ALL is placed in the specification field instead of the number list, all statistics will be reported; if the card is deleted, no statistics will be reported.

9.5 EXAMPLE DECK SETUPS FOR SUBPROGRAM CROSSTABS

Example 9.1 shows the control cards for an SPSS run to produce several tables from the Organizational Membership Study described in Appendix A. The RECODE card is used to collapse the income variable into three broad categories. Two different CROSSTABS requests are used, because different sets of options and statistics are desired for each group of tables.

```
1            16
RUN NAME     CROSSTABS REQUESTS FROM EXAMPLE 9.1
GET FILE     ORGSTUDY
RECODE       INCOME (1 THRU 5 = 1)(6 THRU 41 = 2)(51 THRU 71 = 3)
VALUE LABELS INCOME (1)LOW INCOME(2)MEDIUM INCOME(3)HIGH INCOME
CROSSTABS    TABLES=FRATMEM TO YOUTHMEM BY NATMEM,FARMEM,RELMEM
STATISTICS   1,8
OPTIONS      3
CROSSTABS    TABLES=INCOME BY RELIG, RESDYTH
STATISTICS   ALL
FINISH
```

EXAMPLE 9.1

A total of 21 tables are requested with the first CROSSTABS procedure card (see the DATA LIST card for the ORGSTUDY file in Appendix A to determine the variables included in the FRATMEM TO YOUTHMEM variables list). The STATISTICS card causes the chi-square and gamma statistics to be computed for each table in the first request, and the OPTIONS card causes suppression of row percentages. The first and last table printed by this CROSSTABS request are reproduced in Fig. 9.3.

The second CROSSTABS request specifies two tables, each having the recoded INCOME variable as the row variable. The results appear in Fig. 9.4. Note that none of the processing options were requested. One consequence of this is that all three types of percentages are printed in each cell. The top number in each cell is the absolute frequency count of cases. Immediately below it come the row percentage, the column percentage, and the total percentage, in that order. The items included in each cell and their sequence are reported in the upper left corner of the table for your reference.

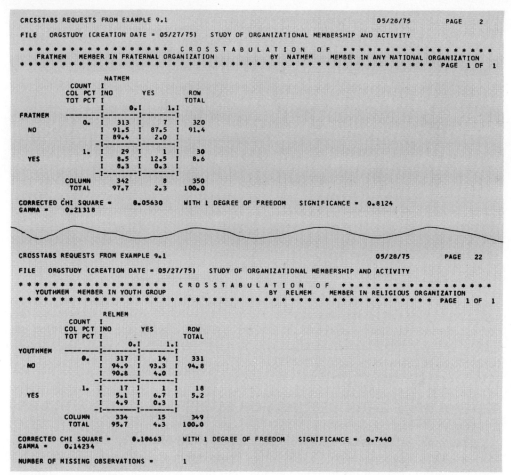

FIGURE 9.3

FIGURE 9.4

```
CROSSTABS REQUESTS FROM EXAMPLE 9.1                              05/28/75    PAGE  25

FILE   ORGSTUDY (CREATION DATE = 05/27/75)   STUDY OF ORGANIZATIONAL MEMBERSHIP AND ACTIVITY

* * * * * * * * * * * * * * * * *   C R O S S T A B U L A T I O N   O F   * * * * * * * * * * * * * * * * *
      INCOME    FAMILY INCOME                              BY  RESDYTH   RESIDENCE DURING FIRST 15 YEARS
* * * * * * * * * * * * * * * * * * * * * * * * * * * * * * * * * * * * * * * * * * *  PAGE  1 OF  1

                         RESDYTH
             COUNT   I
             ROW PCT IMOSTLY F MSTLY SM MSTLY SM MSTLY BI  ROW
             COL PCT IARM     ALL TOWN ALL CITY G CITY,S  TOTAL
             TOT PCT I    1.I     2.I     3.I     4.I
INCOME       --------I--------I--------I--------I--------I
          1. I    58  I    26  I     9  I    17  I   110
 LOW INCOME    I  52.7 I  23.6 I   8.2 I  15.5 I  36.7
               I  58.0 I  29.2 I  28.1 I  21.5 I
               I  19.3 I   8.7 I   3.0 I   5.7 I
             --I--------I--------I--------I--------I
          2. I    39  I    56  I    18  I    51  I   164
 MEDIUM INCOME I  23.8 I  34.1 I  11.0 I  31.1 I  54.7
               I  39.0 I  62.9 I  56.3 I  64.6 I
               I  13.0 I  18.7 I   6.0 I  17.0 I
             --I--------I--------I--------I--------I
          3. I     3  I     7  I     5  I    11  I    26
 HIGH INCOME   I  11.5 I  26.9 I  19.2 I  42.3 I   8.7
               I   3.0 I   7.9 I  15.6 I  13.9 I
               I   1.0 I   2.3 I   1.7 I   3.7 I
             --I--------I--------I--------I--------I
       COLUMN     100       89       32       79      300
       TOTAL     33.3     29.7     10.7     26.3    100.0

CHI SQUARE =    34.44661 WITH   6 DEGREES OF FREEDOM   SIGNIFICANCE =  0.0000
CRAMER'S V =    0.23961
CONTINGENCY COEFFICIENT =    0.32093
LAMBDA (ASYMMETRIC) =  0.13971 WITH INCOME    DEPENDENT.            =  0.12500 WITH RESDYTH  DEPENDENT.
LAMBDA (SYMMETRIC) =  0.13095
UNCERTAINTY COEFFICIENT (ASYMMETRIC) =  0.06316 WITH INCOME    DEPENDENT.         =  0.04365 WITH RESDYTH  DEPENDENT.
UNCERTAINTY COEFFICIENT (SYMMETRIC) =  0.05162
KENDALL'S TAU B =    0.28074 SIGNIFICANCE =  0.0000
KENDALL'S TAU C =    0.26723 SIGNIFICANCE =  0.0000
GAMMA =    0.42943
SOMERS'S D (ASYMMETRIC) =  0.24738 WITH INCOME    DEPENDENT.         =  0.31859 WITH RESDYTH  DEPENDENT.
SOMERS'S D (SYMMETRIC) =  0.27851
ETA =  0.32310 WITH INCOME    DEPENDENT.          =  0.29728 WITH RESDYTH  DEPENDENT.

NUMBER OF MISSING OBSERVATIONS =      50
```

FIGURE 9.4   (continued)

10
SCATTER DIAGRAMS WITH BIVARIATE REGRESSION AND CORRELATION

Crosstabulations help you to study the relationships between two variables only when each variable consists of a relatively small number of discrete values. A different approach is necessary, however, when your variables have been measured at the interval or ratio level and, especially, when there are a large number of different values among the cases. A scatter diagram and a simple regression equation are the most appropriate techniques for investigating such relationships.

Subprogram SCATTERGRAM prints two-variable scatter diagrams (or scattergrams, for short) of data points. The *scattergram* is a two-dimensional plot of points. Figure 10.1(*a*) is a hypothetical example. Each point represents one or more data cases. The coordinates of each point are the values of that case on the two variables being considered. One variable defines the vertical axis of the plot and the other defines the horizontal axis. The resulting pattern of points can tell you a great deal about the relationship between the two variables.

You may use the STATISTICS card with this subprogram to request the statistics associated with simple (i.e., two-variable) regression analysis. These include the regression coefficient and the constant term needed for the regression equation. This equation defines the straight line which best approximates the pattern of points. It may also be used to predict the value of one variable from the other. In addition, a Pearson's correlation coefficient is available from this subprogram. It is a measure of how well the regression line matches the pattern of points, and it may be interpreted as a measure of how strongly the two variables are related.

10.1 REGRESSION, CORRELATION, AND THE SCATTER DIAGRAM

A scattergram presents a "picture" of the relationship between two variables. This picture is analogous to the contingency table printed by the CROSSTABS

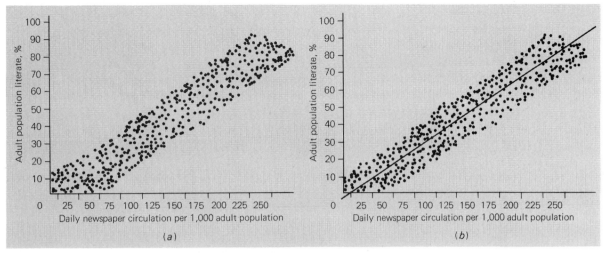

FIGURE 10.1   Scattergram illustrating a strong positive linear relationship.

subprogram. Although contingency tables can be computed with data measured at any level, scattergrams require interval- or ratio-level variables and are more useful when each variable has a great number of distinct values represented among the cases. The variables depicted in Fig. 10.1(*a*) are a good example. Each case has a unique combination of values. A crosstabulation of these data would produce a very large table with most of the cells empty and the others containing only one case. Such a table would not tell us much about the relationship, but the scattergram is very helpful.

The primary statistics used to summarize the relationship depicted in a scattergram are the regression equation and Pearson's correlation coefficient. The *regression equation* is a mathematical formula for predicting the most likely value of one variable from the value of the other variable for a given case. The *correlation coefficient* measures the degree to which the regression equation produces accurate predictions. As such, it is also interpreted as a measure of the strength of association between the two variables. In this section, we will briefly present the use of regression equations and Pearson's correlation coefficient as tools for interpreting scattergrams and understanding bivariate relationships.

As with crosstabulations, scattergrams often suffer from excessive detail. One way to reduce the detail is to draw a straight or curved line through the scattergram in such a manner that it approximates the pattern of points. Thus, in Fig. 10.1(*a*), the rate of adult literacy seems to have a strong positive relationship to newspaper circulation. This is because the points cluster in a narrow band forming a pattern that could be well summarized by a straight line drawn through the scatter of data points. This has been done in Fig. 10.1(*b*). In contrast, there does not appear to be any systematic relationship among the data represented in Fig. 10.2(*a*), because the points do not show any distinct pattern. A mild degree of clustering along a downward-sloping straight line seems present in Fig. 10.2(*b*), which indicates a moderate degree of negative association. The pattern in Fig. 10.2(*c*) is very distinct and indicates a fairly high degree of association based on a curvilinear relationship.

If we can find a line with known mathematical properties to represent the general

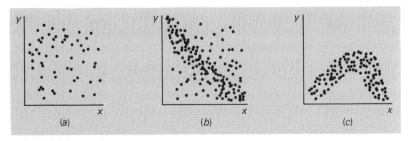

FIGURE 10.2   Scattergrams illustrating different types of relationships.

data pattern in a scatter diagram, then the formula for that line can serve as a *summary* of the relationship between the two variables. In addition, the closer the data points fall to the line that best summarizes the relationship, the stronger the correlation between the two variables.

The most common statistical procedure for fitting a line to a scattergram based on interval-level variables is called *least-squares regression*. This method is based on the belief that the best-fitting line is the one where the vertical distances of all the points from the line are minimized. The line itself is called the regression line.

If we draw a straight or curved line through a scattergram, any point which does not fall exactly on the line is not completely accounted for. By not drawing the line through the point, we have committed an "error," and the amount of error is the vertical distance from the point to the line. The sum of the error distances squared is a measure of the total error involved when the regression line is used as the prediction of the location of the data points. A line which minimizes this sum of squared distances will serve as a better predictor than any other line. If variable Y is plotted along the vertical axis and variable X along the horizontal, we would call the resulting line the regression of Y on X, because the vertical distances are being minimized. If we were to compute the regression of X on Y, we would have to minimize the horizontal distances, and our result would usually be a very different line.

The objective of linear regression is to locate the best-fitting *straight* line. Linear regression is the most common type used, because it gives a simple summary of the relationship and because most variables of interest to social scientists are assumed to be related in a straight-line manner. Thus, the linear regression equation is the same as the general formula for a straight line:

$$Y = a + bX$$

Here, the value a is called the *intercept* and is the value of variable Y at the point where the line crosses the Y (vertical) axis (the value of X is zero there). The coefficient b is the *slope* of the line. It denotes how much Y changes for a 1-unit change in X. When the values of a and b are determined by the least squares regression method, b is called the *regression coefficient*. In statistical terminology, Y is the *dependent variable* and X is the *independent variable*. The SCATTERGRAM subprogram computes the linear regression coefficient and the intercept when you request them on the STATISTICS card.

Sometimes a bivariate relationship, such as that shown in Fig. 10.2(c), is more aptly described by a curve. Regression methods for fitting a curve are called *curvilinear* or *polynomial regression*. The criterion of least-squares distances still applies, but the formula derived looks somewhat different. The SCATTERGRAM subprogram is not useful for curvilinear regression, but you may use the REGRESSION subprogram in that situation. The REGRESSION subprogram is also helpful when you want to compute a regression equation involving more than one independent variable. See the SPSS manual for details.

In most social science research, you are unlikely to find a regression line, especially a straight one, which perfectly fits the data. Whether this is because the true relationship does not quite fit the curve being drawn or because of errors or imprecision in collecting the data, we need some measure of the "goodness of fit" of the regression line. The *Pearson product-moment correlation coefficient*, symbolized by the letter r, serves this purpose for *linear* regression. When there is a perfect fit (no error), r takes on the value of $+1.0$ or -1.0. The sign of r is the same as the sign of the regression coefficient and indicates the direction of the slope. A negative r does not mean a bad fit. Rather, it denotes an inverse relationship. Figure 10.2(b) is an example of an inverse relationship—as X becomes larger, Y tends to become smaller. A positive correlation means that X and Y tend to increase together, as depicted in Fig. 10.1. When the linear regression line is a poor fit to the data, r will be close to zero. Indeed, the value of zero denotes the absence of a *linear* relationship, as seems to be the case for Figs. 10.2(a) and (c).

Pearson's *r* serves a dual purpose. Besides its role as an indicator of the "goodness of fit" of the linear regression, it is also a measure of association which tells us the strength of the linear relationship existing between the two variables. The regression coefficient *b* does not serve either purpose; it merely represents the mathematical slope of the line. When we want to know the strength and direction of a linear relationship, we must consult *r*. If the value of *r* is close to zero, we can assume there is little or no *linear* relationship between the two variables. If the value of *r* approaches +1.0 or −1.0, we can assume there is a strong *linear* relationship. If *r* is somewhere in between, say +.5 or −.5, the relationship is moderate.

When we square the Pearson *r* statistic, we obtain another statistic denoted by r^2. (The range of r^2 goes from a minimum of 0 to a maximum of 1.0.) Actually, we can more easily interpret r^2 as a measure of association when our concern is with the strength of relationship rather than the direction of relationship. This is because r^2 is a measure of the proportion of variance in one variable "explained" by the other.

Variance is a measure of the variability, or lack of homogeneity, in a variable (see Sec. 8.1 for more details). When the cases cluster close to the mean, variance will be small, but as the cases become more spread out, variance increases. The objective of correlation analysis is to determine the extent to which variation in one variable is linked to variation in the other, which we refer to as *concomitant variation*.

Concomitant variation of one variable with another "explains" variance in the following sense. If we want to predict the value of some variable *Y* (for example, the percentage of the adult population which is literate) for a given country without having any other knowledge of the country's characteristics, our best guess would be the average (mean) literacy figure for all the countries. The variance of *Y* gives an indication of how far off our prediction is likely to be, because it is based on the sum of squared distances of the cases from the mean of the variable. Now, if we find some characteristic *X* (for instance, daily newspaper circulation) of these countries which happens to be linearly correlated with *Y*, our ability to predict the level of literacy will be improved. The prediction strategy is to compute the regression line and to predict that the value of *Y* (literacy) is the point on the regression line corresponding to the country's position on *X* (newspaper circulation). Thus, if we knew that a particular country had a newspaper circulation of 100 per 1,000 adults, a regression line to fit the data depicted in Fig. 10.1 would predict a literacy rate of about 20 percent. Yet, clearly, the several countries with this level of newspaper circulation have actual literacy rates ranging from about 10 percent to 30 percent. If there is a high correlation, as measured by *r*, most of the data points will fall very close to the line, and the differences (errors) between our predictions and the true values will be much smaller on the average than the discrepancy which would occur by always predicting the mean value of *Y*.

We can use the amount of these errors to measure the degree of remaining variance, which is called the *residual variance*. *Residual variance* is the amount of original (total) variance which cannot be "explained" by using the regression line as a prediction device. Residual variance will never be greater than total variance, and the proportion to which it is less is the proportion of variance explained (r^2)—i.e.,

$$r^2 = \frac{\text{total variance} - \text{residual variance}}{\text{total variance}}$$

Unlike the regression coefficient, *r* and r^2 are symmetric measures of association. When using them, it really does not matter which variable we consider to be predicting the other, because both *r* and r^2 measure the strength of the *linear* relationship.

Subprogram SCATTERGRAM computes yet another statistic called the standard error of the estimate of the slope, which is useful when working with data from a sample. Briefly stated, the standard error is a measure of the confidence we can have that *b* represents the true regression slope in the population from which the sample was drawn. A fuller explanation of the standard error is beyond the scope of this primer, but advanced statistics texts dealing with regression analysis can give you further details.

10.2 SCATTERGRAM PROCEDURE CARD

The SCATTERGRAM procedure card contains the keyword SCAT-TERGRAM in the control field starting in column 1. The specification field contains the variable names for the variables you want to plot.

The specification field can have two different formats. The first of these consists merely of a variable list. If you choose this format, you may use all of the usual SPSS conventions in naming the variables to be included (see Secs. 5.5 and 6.1.). An example employing variables from the COMSTUDY file follows:

```
1               16
SCATTERGRAM     MEDSCH TO PTMANU, WHTCOLAR
```

This format will result in a separate plot for every possible *pair* of variables given in the list. In the above example, this amounts to 15 plots, because there are 15 unique pairs of variables that could be made from the six variables referenced by the variable list. The first plot for the above example will show the relationship between MEDSCH as the vertical variable and MEDFINC as the horizontal variable, the second plot would be MEDSCH and PTGOHS, and so on, until MEDSCH and WHTCOLAR. Then the next plot will have MEDFINC as the vertical variable and PTGOHS as the horizontal variable, and so on, until the entire variable list is exhausted. For each pair of variables, the first one named determines the vertical axis and the second determines the horizontal axis.

In the second format style, the keyword WITH is used to create plots only between variables appearing before and after the keyword WITH. The variable lists on both sides of the keyword WITH follow normal SPSS conventions; for example:

```
1               16
SCATTERGRAM     MEDSCH MEDFINC WITH PTGOHS TO PTMANU
```

This specification will produce six plots: MEDSCH along the vertical axis with PTGOHS along the horizontal axis, MEDSCH with PTAGRI, MEDSCH with PTMANU, MEDFINC with PTGOHS, MEDFINC with PTAGRI, and MED-FINC with PTMANU. Each variable to the left of the WITH is paired with each variable to the right. The variables on the left are used to define the vertical axis (which is the dependent variable in the regression equation), and those on the right define the horizontal axis (which is the independent variable in the regression equation).

If not differently specified, the scales on the axes are determined by the lowest and highest values of each variable in the plot. Thus, if the range of a particular variable is from 6 through 49, the axis would begin at 6 and end at 49 for that variable.

You may change this range, however, if you wish to have different beginning and ending values. This is desirable in two situations. Suppose you have a variable, such as WHTCOLAR from the ORGSTUDY, where the lowest value is 1 and the highest is 71. If you feel that the plot would be easier to understand with the axis extending from 0 to 100, you may specify that range. Alternatively, you may have a variable with a few cases at extreme values but almost all of the other cases clustered in a narrow range. A plot with that variable would show many cases tightly clustered in one area with a few cases far away at the edge. You can omit the extreme cases, by giving a narrow value range which excludes those values. The result would be a plot with the remaining points more fully dispersed about the page, because a smaller range can be spread over the same-length axis.[1] The number of cases excluded from the plot because their values fall outside the specified range is printed beneath the plot.

---

[1] An alternate strategy for the latter situation is to recode the extreme values to some value closer to the other points. Because both strategies have important statistical implications, you should employ them with care.

The exact format to specify a new range of values after the variable name is: left parenthesis [(], lowest value or the keyword LOWEST, highest value or the keyword HIGHEST, right parenthesis [)]. You can use the keywords LOWEST and HIGHEST to specify a range from the lowest value read in to any chosen value, or from any chosen value to the highest value read in. As an example, the specification (0,100) would be used to force the axis to begin at 0 and end at 100. The specification (LOWEST, 53) would cause the axis to begin at the lowest value read in and end with the value 53.

A value-range specification applies only to the *immediately preceding* variable in the variable list. If you gave the specification PTMANU, PTTERTRY (0,100), the value range would affect only the variable PTTERTRY; PTMANU would be plotted in the usual fashion. Therefore, if you want to use the value-range specifications on a series of variable names or a variables list for which you would normally use the TO convention, you must enter each variable name and its associated value range separately. This rule is illustrated in the following example:

```
1                16
SCATTERGRAM      MEDSCH(0,10) WITH WHTCOLAR (7,HIGHEST) PTGOHS
                 TO PTMANU (LOWEST,99)/
```

The scale for variable MEDSCH will have the lowest value of zero and the highest value of 10, WHTCOLAR will go from 7 to the highest value read in. The scales for PTGOHS and PTAGRI are determined by the lowest and highest value encountered, since no value range is specifically given for them. PTMANU will have a range from the lowest value read in up to 99. If you want the range (LOWEST, 99) to apply to PTGOHS and PTAGRI, too, you would have to enter the specification as follows:

```
1                16
SCATTERGRAM      MEDSCH(0,10) WITH WHTCOLAR (7, HIGHEST) PTGOHS(LOWEST,99)
                 PTAGRI(LOWEST,99) PTMANU(LOWEST,99)
```

The general format of the SCATTERGRAM procedure card is

or

With either format, the first request for plots may be followed by a slash and then another request. You can repeat the pattern of request, slash, request, slash, etc., up to 25 times.

When you make multiple requests, you can intermix both formats. The following examples, taken from the COMSTUDY file reported in Appendix A, illustrate this intermixture.

```
1               16
SCATTERGRAM     MEDSCH WITH HRSWORK TO PARTISAN/   MEDSCH HRSWORK (2,6)
SCATTERGRAM     WHTCOLAR WITH LIFE TIME NEWSWEEK READDIG/
                MEDFINC WITH HRSWORK (LOWEST, 6) WHTCOLAR/
```

The first part of the first SCATTERGRAM control card results in four plots, one for every variable to the right of the keyword WITH with the variable MEDSCH; for the second part, one plot is generated showing the variables MEDSCH and HRSWORK where the latter has a value range from 2 to 6. For the first part of the second SCAT-TERGRAM control card, four plots are printed which show the relationship between WHTCOLAR and LIFE, TIME, NEWSWEEK, and READDIG. For the second part of the control card, two plots are generated. The scale for HRSWORK goes from the lowest value read up to the value 6.

10.3 OPTIONS AVAILABLE FOR SUBPROGRAM SCATTERGRAM

Subprogram SCATTERGRAM offers you eight options. If you choose any of them, you should enter their identifying numbers on an OPTIONS control card which will directly follow the SCATTERGRAM control card or the STATISTICS card. The options are as follows.

OPTION 1 All missing values are included in the plots and in the statistical calculations specified on the STATISTICS card.

OPTION 2 Missing values are excluded from the plot and from the statistics in a listwise fashion. This means that a case is deleted if any of the variables in the SCATTERGRAM variable list has a missing value.

OPTION 3 Suppresses the printing of variable labels.

OPTION 4 Suppresses the plot grid lines. When present, these lines run parallel to the vertical and horizontal axes and divide the graph into nine almost equal sections for easier location of specific plots.

OPTION 5 Prints diagonal grids.

OPTION 6 Makes a two-tailed test of significance if you choose statistic 3.

OPTION 7 Produces automatic scaling. This option produces integer plot scales. The lowest scale value is set to the largest integer which is less than or equal to the lowest value encountered in the data. The highest value is set to the smallest integer which is (1) larger than or equal to the highest value encountered in the data, and (2) for the variable on the vertical axis = the lowest scale value $+10n$; or for the variable on the horizontal axis = the lowest scale value $+20m$ (n and m are the lowest possible positive integers necessary to set the upper scale value greater than or equal to the highest data value).

Note: If you specify a range for a particular variable and also select option 7, the specified range will override option 7.

OPTION 8 If insufficient work space is available to process all the cases in the file, the plots will be produced nevertheless and will include the first n cases, where n is the maximum number that may be produced.

If no OPTIONS control card is included in the deck setup, the following default options are in force:

(*a*) Cases with missing data will be deleted in a pairwise fashion. This means a case is deleted from the plot if one of the two variables in *that plot* is missing.

(*b*) Variable labels are printed after the variable name on top of the graph.

(*c*) Rectangular plot grid lines are printed.

(*d*) A one-tailed test of significance is made if statistic 3 is chosen.

(*e*) No automatic scaling is done.

(*f*) No plots will be produced for the file (or the subfile group) if not enough core storage space is available to process all cases.

10.4 STATISTICS AVAILABLE FOR SUBPROGRAM SCATTERGRAM

To obtain any of the available statistics, place the appropriate reference number on the STATISTICS control card. This card should come directly after the OPTIONS control card; or, if no OPTIONS card is used, it should come directly behind the SCATTERGRAM control card. The reference numbers of the available statistics are:

STATISTIC 1   Pearson's *r* (product-moment correlation coefficient)

STATISTIC 2   *r*-squared

STATISTIC 3   Significance of *r*

STATISTIC 4   Standard error of the estimate

STATISTIC 5   Intercept with the vertical axis, *a*

STATISTIC 6   Slope, *b*

If you want to see all the available statistics, place the keyword ALL in the specification field of the STATISTICS control card.

10.5 SAMPLE DECK SETUP AND OUTPUT FOR SUBPROGRAM SCATTERGRAM

Example 10.1 illustrates the use of subprogram SCATTERGRAM in a run using an SPSS system file. The first execution of SCATTERGRAM produces two plots. Figure 10.3 shows the first of these. The variable WHTCOLAR defines the vertical axis and option 7 requests integer scaling. But because the procedure card specifies the upper and lower limits for MEDSCH, option 7 does not apply to this variable. The values of 6 and 16 will cause integer scaling to appear along the bottom horizontal edge of the graph. Note that automatic integer scaling for this variable would not have been very desirable, because it would have forced the range to extend from 6 through 26. This would have resulted in the points being crowded into the left-hand portion of the

```
1               16
RUN NAME        SCATTERGRAMS PRODUCED BY EXAMPLE 10.1
GET FILE        COMSTUDY
SCATTERGRAM     WHTCOLAR WITH MEDSCH (6,16), MEDFINC
OPTIONS         7
STATISTICS      ALL
SCATTERGRAM     POP60 (0,64000), POPLAT(0,64000)
OPTIONS         4,5
STATISTICS      ALL
FINISH
```

EXAMPLE 10.1

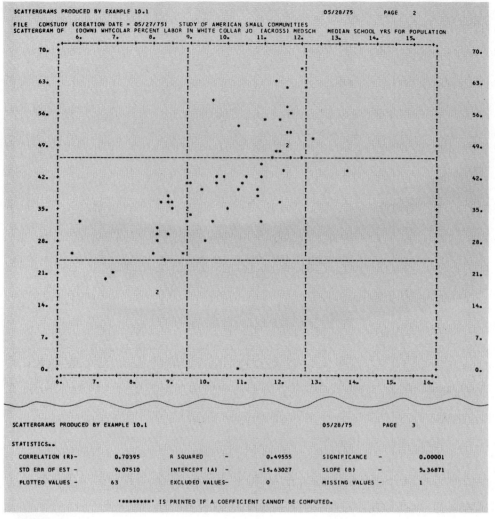

FIGURE 10.3

graph. Of course, when neither automatic scaling nor the specification of upper and lower limits is made, SPSS uses the default scaling procedure. The statistics are not influenced by the scaling feature used except when the specification of upper and lower limits forces cases to be excluded.

In Fig. 10.3 each asterisk denotes a unique data point—a single community, in this instance. The 2 which occurs in the lower left-hand corner denotes that two communities had equal or nearly equal values on both variables. If two through eight cases fall into the same position, the actual number of cases is printed. Nine *or more* cases are represented by the number 9. Because each printing position represents a small rectangle of territory, points that are not exactly identical may still be included in the same printing position if they are sufficiently similar.

The second execution of the SCATTERGRAM subprogram illustrates the use of diagonal grid lines while suppressing the horizontal and vertical grid lines. The resulting plot appears in Fig. 10.4.

You will find scatter diagrams most useful when the data points are scattered about the plot rather than clustered in only a few positions. Variables with a wide variety of values tend to produce a broad scattering of points. Figure 10.3 is a good example. Because very few communities have the same proportion of the labor force in white-collar jobs and the same median school years for the population over 25, almost every community falls in a unique position in the plot. In contrast, a scattergram based on the variables GOVSELCT and CONELECT would show you very little variation.

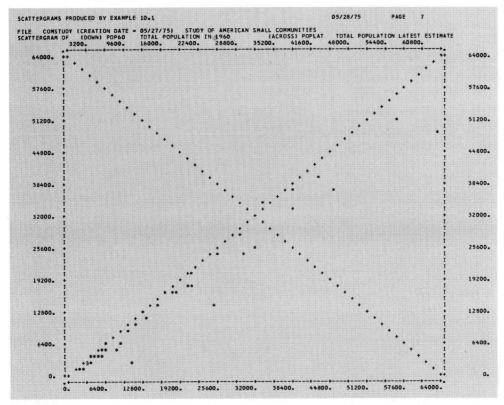

FIGURE 10.4

At the most, you would see 16 points corresponding to the 16 possible combinations of categories in the two variables. Because of the limited possibilities, many communities would share the same position. As a result, you would find it difficult to identify a meaningful relationship between those two variables. When you find yourself in such a situation, you should have SPSS produce a crosstabulation instead.

11
COMPARISON OF SAMPLE MEANS WITH THE T-TEST

A type of analysis often encountered in social research is the comparison of sample means on some given interval- or ratio-level variable. The statistical question to be answered is whether the two means are significantly different or if the similarity is so close that there is a reasonable probability that the means do not differ in the larger population. The statistical procedure commonly employed to answer this question is Student's *t*-test.

Subprogram T-TEST provides the capability of computing the Student's *t* statistic and its associated probability level. The test may be applied to the difference between two means derived from either of two sources:

1 Measurements on the same variable for two independent samples. Here, each case is a member of only one of the two groups, and a test of mean differences between the groups is made for one specified variable. An example would be to test the differences in mean IQ scores for a group of white children versus a group of black children. This form of the *t*-test is referred to as the "independent samples" *t*-test.
2 Measurements on two different variables taken on the same cases. Here, there is only one sample, but the same cases are measured twice in some fashion. This could be two different measurements taken at the same time, such as two different IQ tests, or the same measurement taken at different times, such as the same IQ test given at the beginning and the end of the school year. This form of the *t*-test is referred to as the "paired samples" or "correlated" *t*-test.

11.1 STATISTICAL INFERENCE FROM A SAMPLE OF CASES

In statistical research, we are often concerned with comparing the measurements for one group with those of another to see if the groups are different. When the measurement has been made with a nominal- or ordinal-level variable, we would most likely use a contingency table to compare the group distributions. If the variable in question has been measured at the interval or ratio level, however, we can easily check for a difference by comparing the means for each group.

Our comparison of group means is very straightforward when the cases constitute the entire population under investigation. Then any observed difference is a real difference, at least to the extent that we have accurately measured the variable. For instance, we might want to compare the support of social welfare legislation among Republican and Democratic Senators during 1974. Because there are only 100 Senators, we would not find it too difficult to count the number of social welfare bills supported by each Senator. If we found that the average Republican Senator supported 35 bills and the average Democratic Senator supported 56, there would be no question that the Democrats were more favorable to social welfare legislation.

When our data cases are only a sample from the total population, however, we must contend with an extra problem. This is the possibility that our sample consists of cases that by chance are not really representative of the population. Such a biased sample would not, of course, represent the true distribution of cases in the population. Going back to our Senate example, let us say we randomly selected only five Senators from each party in order to reduce the amount of work in the study. Even if the mean support for each party was again 35 bills to 56, we would not be certain that this represents a true difference between the parties. (Remember that we are ignorant of the true difference this time, because we did not study every Senator.) *Perhaps* there is no real difference between the parties and we just happened to select only Republicans who were unusually opposed to social welfare and Democrats who were unusually supportive of such legislation. This is an unlikely event, but the important thing is that *it is possible,* especially with a small sample.

Before making the inference that our sample difference represents a real difference in the population, we should compute the probability that the difference occurred due to chance. If this probability is very low, say 1 in 20 (.05) or 1 in 100 (.01), then we would be willing to take the risk of saying that our sample reflects a true difference. When the probability is higher, the risk of drawing a wrong conclusion is higher. These probabilities never *prove* the presence or absence of a difference in the population. They merely advise us about the likelihood of obtaining a difference as large as or larger than the one observed in our sample when there is actually no difference in the population.

When we have a low probability level, we say that the difference is statistically significant. Researchers typically use the values of .05, .01, and .001 as cutoff points, depending upon how cautious they want to be. But these values are not sacred. Because significance tests are greatly influenced by the sample size, they tell us primarily whether the sample was sufficiently large to accurately detect any difference.

You should not confuse a statistically significant difference with a substantively meaningful difference. A small difference may turn out to be statistically significant, but the magnitude may be too small to be important. For instance, if we found that the average number of social welfare bills supported by Republicans was 45 compared with 46 for Democrats, we would not be impressed. This may be a real difference, but it is not important in explaining Senatorial behavior or policy outcomes.

11.1.1 T-TEST FOR COMPARISONS OF INDEPENDENT SAMPLES

When we wish to evaluate the statistical significance of a difference between two sample means, we often use a statistical procedure known as the *t*-test. The *t*-test, of course, requires that the measurements have been made with an interval- or ratio-level variable (otherwise, the mean would not be an appropriate statistic). It also assumes that the variable is normally distributed in the population.

The first step in using the *t*-test is to compute a statistic referred to as Student's *t*. The value of *t* itself is not important, but we can use it to determine the probability associated with the observed difference of means. This is so because statisticians have worked out formulas which translate *t* into the corresponding probability level. These formulas also require a number known as the *degrees of freedom* for the samples. In this context, the degrees of freedom adjust the probability formulas for the sizes of your samples.

The formulas and computations involved are sometimes complicated. The SPSS manual and many statistics texts explain them in detail. Fortunately for you, SPSS does all the work and prints out the values of *t,* the degrees of freedom, and the probability. You need only decide whether the results are significant for your purposes.

Let us consider the results printed in Fig. 11.1 as an example. This printout was based on data from the ORGSTUDY file. White respondents (group 1) are being compared with nonwhite respondents (group 2) on three variables: NMEM, NACT, and AGE. The left-hand portion of the printout reports the number of cases, the means, the standard deviation, and the standard error on the given variable for each group. These are the building blocks for the remaining computations. In the center you will find printed an *F* value and its associated probability. Before explaining the rest of the printout, we must digress to an explanation of this *F* value.

The traditional *t*-test assumes that the two samples are drawn from populations with equal variances on the variable being studied. (*Variance* is a statistic which measures how closely the cases cluster about the mean. It is equal to the standard deviation squared.) As the result of chance differences in the samples, you are not likely to find exactly equal sample variances even if the population variances are equal. You can, however, test your assumption that sample variances are sufficiently similar. This is where the *F* value comes in. It is a statistical test for the equality of the group variances. If the *F* value is *not* significant (i.e., if the associated probability is *larger* than some cutoff value, such as .05), then you may use the regular *t*-test formula. This formula averages the sample variances in a special way to obtain a "pooled variance estimate." If the *F* value is significant (i.e., if the associated probability is *smaller* than some cutoff value), then you would assume that the differences in the sample variances reflect real differences in the corresponding populations. In this situation, the value of *t* can only be approximated, and SPSS uses a different formula which incorporates the separate estimates of the variance.

Once you have interpreted the *F* value, you can decide which portion of the printout gives the *t*-test appropriate for your data. As you can see, on the right side of Fig. 11.1 there is one portion labelled "pooled variance estimate" and another labelled "separate variance estimate." For the variable NMEM, the *F* value has a rather high probability (.625), which indicates that the sample variances are sufficiently similar. Therefore, we would use the *t* value reported under pooled variance estimate. This *t* value is equal to 1.75 and has a significance level of .082. Most researchers would not consider this sufficiently small to be significant. Thus, we would say that there is an 8.2 percent probability that the white and nonwhite means (1.0288 versus .7500) for

PRINTOUT FOR FIGURE 11.1   05/28/75   PAGE   2

FILE   ORGSTUDY (CREATION DATE = 05/27/75)   STUDY OF ORGANIZATIONAL MEMBERSHIP AND ACTIVITY

- T - T E S T -

GROUP 1 - RACE   EQ   1.
GROUP 2 - RACE   EQ   2.

VARIABLE	NUMBER OF CASES	MEAN	STANDARD DEVIATION	STANDARD ERROR	POOLED VARIANCE ESTIMATE			SEPARATE VARIANCE ESTIMATE		
					F VALUE	2-TAIL PROB.	T VALUE	DEGREES OF FREEDOM	2-TAIL PROB.	T VALUE	DEGREES OF FREEDOM	2-TAIL PROB.
NMEM												
GROUP 1	278	1.0288	1.219	0.073	1.11	0.625	1.75	348	0.082	1.80	115.05	0.075
GROUP 2	72	0.7500	1.160	0.137								
NACT												
GROUP 1	278	0.5108	0.809	0.049	1.85	0.001	0.21	348	0.832	0.18	91.83	0.859
GROUP 2	72	0.4861	1.100	0.130								
AGE												
GROUP 1	278	45.1655	17.342	1.040	1.26	0.239	0.43	348	0.670	0.46	121.75	0.648
GROUP 2	72	44.2083	15.425	1.818								

FIGURE 11.1

number of memberships would differ by that much or more when they are really equal in the total population.

In contrast, the *F* value for NACT is statistically significant, because its probability is only .001. Therefore, we must use the *t* value reported under separate variance estimate. Here, the *t* value is .18 with a .859 probability. This probability is very large and definitely not statistically significant. Indeed, the means (.5108 for whites versus .4861 for nonwhites) are very close.

11.1.2 T-TEST FOR PAIRED COMPARISONS

In the discussion so far, we have been talking about comparisons of means on a single variable between two different samples. These samples must have been drawn randomly, and the selection of cases for one sample must have been completely independent of the selection process for the other sample. Because of the independent sampling, we refer to the *t*-test used in that situation as the *independent samples t-test*.

Another frequently used *t*-test is the *paired samples t-test*, also known as the *correlated t*. We use this test when we want to compare the means on two variables from the same sample. These variables may have been two characteristics measured at the same point in time, such as the sales of *Time Magazine* and of *Newsweek* in American small communities. Or, you may be comparing the same characteristic measured on the same cases at two different points in time, such as community population in 1960 with the latest population estimate. Another example is the comparison of "pre-test" results to "post-test" results with some sort of experimental treatment coming in between.

These two different situations—independent samples versus paired samples—require different formulas for the *t*-test. Therefore, you must tell SPSS which situation applies to your data, as we will discuss later in the chapter. The procedure for interpreting the results is basically the same in both situations, with two minor exceptions. When using the paired *t*-test, you should check the correlation between the two variables to be certain that it is positive. A negative correlation indicates a contradictory pattern of changes. Then, instead of comparing the variable means, you should seek to explain the negative correlation. In addition, a paired *t*-test always uses a pooled estimate of the variance. So, you need not consider whether to use a pooled or separate variance estimate as is necessary with independent samples.

Figure 11.2 gives an example of SPSS printout for a paired *t*-test. The data are from the COMSTUDY file with POP60 being compared with POPLAT. On the left, the printout reports the number of cases and the mean, standard deviation, and standard error of the mean for each variable. In the center, you can find the mean difference of cases (the second variable subtracted from the first) and the standard deviation and standard error of the differences for each case. The third column reports the correlation between the variables and its probability level (i.e., the probability of finding a sample correlation this large or larger due to chance when there is no correlation in the population). As you can see, the correlation for these variables is positive, so we can go on to examine the *t* value. This is reported on the far right. In this instance, the value of *t* is −3.61 with 38 degrees of freedom. The corresponding probability level is .001, which is

VARIABLE	NUMBER OF CASES	MEAN	STANDARD DEVIATION	STANDARD ERROR	*(DIFFERENCE) MEAN	STANDARD DEVIATION	STANDARD ERROR	* 2-TAIL CORR. PROB.	* T VALUE	DEGREES OF FREEDOM	2-TAIL PROB.
POP60	TOTAL POPULATION IN 1960										
		16614.4609	13921.004	2229.145							
	39				-1936.3047	3347.980	536.106	0.982 0.000	-3.61	38	0.001
		18550.7656	15739.473	2520.333							
POPLAT	TOTAL POPULATION LATEST ESTIMATE										

FIGURE 11.2

statistically significant. Thus, we can be very safe in concluding that the observed increase in population is not merely due to sampling error.

11.1.3 ONE-TAILED TESTS VERSUS TWO-TAILED TESTS OF SIGNIFICANCE

All of the printouts from subprogram T-TEST report "two-tailed probabilities" when giving the significance level. This jargon refers to the method of computing probabilities from the theoretical t distribution. What this means for you is that no assumptions have been made about which mean is larger than the other. Rather, your statistical concern is whether there is *any* difference at all. The same applies to the F test for equal variances (Is *either* variance larger?) and the paired variables correlation (Is it at all different from zero, either positively or negatively?).

If you want to test whether one particular mean is larger than the other, then you should use a one-tailed test of significance. This would have been appropriate when comparing POP60 with POPLAT. Our expectation is that the population has grown, so the mean for POPLAT should be greater than the mean for POP60. Notice how this is different from saying we will accept any difference, because that would lead us to be satisfied with a population *decrease* as well as an increase.

It is very easy to obtain a one-tailed test of significance for the t value. You merely take the reported two-tailed probability and divide by 2. Thus, in Fig. 11.2, the one-tailed test for a comparison of POP60 with POPLAT would yield a .0005 probability level. Of course, you should check the direction of the difference of means first. If the wrong mean is larger, then there is no need to do a t-test, because your hypothesized difference is obviously not there.

11.2 T-TEST PROCEDURE CARD

To call subprogram T-TEST, place the control word T-TEST in columns 1 to 6 of a procedure card. In the specification field, beginning in column 16, list the variables you want tested and the type of test.

Two types of tests may be performed using T-TEST. First, you may test the difference in means of a given variable between two distinct groups of cases (independent samples t-test). The format of the T-TEST procedure card for this type of test is presented in Sec. 11.2.1. Alternatively, you may test the difference in the means of two variables, each measured on all the cases being processed (paired t-test). Instructions for preparing the appropriate T-TEST procedure card for this type of paired samples test are given in Sec. 11.2.2.

11.2.1 TESTS BETWEEN GROUPS (INDEPENDENT SAMPLES)

For tests between groups, the specification field of the T-TEST procedure card identifies the groups and variables you are testing. The general format of the control card is:

1	16
T-TEST	GROUPS=group specification/VARIABLES= $\begin{cases} \text{variable name} \\ \text{or} \\ \text{variable list} \end{cases}$

The group specification may be communicated in any of three different ways. When using the format

GROUPS=varname (value)/

group 1 is formed by all cases where the value of variable "varname" is greater than or equal to "value." Group 2 consists of the remaining cases. An alternative format is to give the specification as

GROUPS=varname (value1, value2)/

Group 1 consists of all cases where the value of variable varname is equal to value1; group 2 consists of all cases where the value of variable varname is equal to value2. All other cases are ignored. The special case where value1 = 1.0 and value2 = 2.0 may be specified as:

GROUPS=varname/

Finally, the groups may be specified according to their sizes in the following manner:

GROUPS=n_1,n_2/

The groups are formed by taking the first n_1 cases as group 1 and the next n_2 cases as group 2. Naturally, all the cases for group 1 must come first in the file, followed by all the cases from group 2, when this format is used.

Following the group specification, you punch a slash [/], then the keyword VARIA-BLES=, and, finally, a variable name or variable list of the usual type. A separate *t*-test will be performed for each variable in the variable list. The variables are *not* compared with one another. Rather, the mean for each variable is computed for the first group and the second group; then the two means on the same variable are tested.

The following control cards illustrate the format of the T-TEST procedure card for tests between groups.

```
1                16
T-TEST           GROUPS = 27, 39/ VARIABLES = VAR001
T-TEST           GROUPS = RACE/ VARIABLES=EDUC, INCOME
T-TEST           GROUPS = AGE(40)/ VARIABLES = POLATT1 TO POLATT10
```

On the first card, the mean of VAR001 over the first 27 cases is compared with the mean of VAR001 over the next 39 cases. Two separate tests are requested on the second card. First, the mean level of EDUC for RACE category 1 is tested against the mean level of EDUC for RACE category 2. Then, the same two racial groups are tested for differences on the INCOME variable. In the third example, the cases are divided into groups according to their value on the AGE variable. The first group consists of persons 40 years old or older, while the second group is comprised of all persons younger than 40. Separate *t*-tests are to be computed for each variable in the file beginning with POLATT1 and ending with POLATT10.

11.2.2 TESTS BETWEEN VARIABLES (PAIRED SAMPLES)

You may specify paired *t*-tests with this format:

```
1                16
T-TEST           PAIRS= {variable name  [WITH {variable name ]/...
                         or                     or
                        variable list}          variable list}
```

Following the keyword PAIRS=, you simply enter a variable list if you wish to test the mean differences between every possible pair of variables in the list. Alternatively, you may enter a variable name or variable list, then the keyword WITH, and finally another variable name or list. This latter format allows you to test only the mean differences between each variable in the left-hand list with each variable in the right-hand list. This format is similar to the one used on the SCATTERGRAM procedure card (except that upper and lower limits may not be specified here).

You can enter multiple requests by placing a slash [/] following a variable list (or combination of variable list WITH variable list) and then entering another variable list (or variable list WITH variable list combination).

The following control cards illustrate the format of the T-TEST procedure card for tests between variables. Note that these procedure cards will all generate the same three tests.

```
1               16
T-TEST          PAIRS = TIME1 WITH TIME2/ TIME1 WITH TIME3/ TIME1 WITH TIME4
T-TEST          PAIRS = TIME1, TIME2/ TIME1, TIME3/ TIME1,TIME4
T-TEST          PAIRS = TIME1 WITH TIME2 TO TIME4
```

In each of these examples, the mean for variable TIME1 will be computed over *all* the cases and tested against the mean of variable TIME2 computed over all the cases. Similar tests will be made with the TIME1 mean compared with the TIME3 mean and the TIME1 mean compared with the TIME4 mean. In each instance, all the cases are used in computing the means, except for cases omitted because of missing values.

11.2.3 REQUESTING BOTH TYPES OF TESTS IN ONE T-TEST TASK

You can request both types of *t*-test, between groups and between variables, on the same T-TEST procedure card. The GROUPS= specification must appear first, followed by the VARIABLES= list to define the desired between-groups tests. Follow this with the PAIRS= lists. An example is:

```
1               16
T-TEST          GROUPS = GOVSELCT (2,3)/ VARIABLES = MEDSCH, MEDFINC, WHTCOLAR
                TO READDIG/
                PAIRS = POP60 WITH POPLAT/ LIFE TO READDIG
```

You can request both types of *t*-test, between groups and between variables, on once on a T-TEST procedure card. The between-variables tests (i.e., PAIRS=) will always be performed using all the cases from all the groups. This is true even when between-groups tests (i.e., GROUPS= with VARIABLES=) are performed during the same task.

11.3 OPTIONS AND STATISTICS FOR SUBPROGRAM T-TEST

If you desire any of the special processing options, you may follow the T-TEST procedure card with an OPTIONS card. The available options are as follows.

OPTION 1   *Inclusion of missing data.* This option causes missing value indicators to be ignored and enters all data into the computations.

OPTION 2   *Listwise deletion of missing data.* This option causes omission of a case from the analysis if *any* variable on the VARIABLES= list or the PAIRS= list contains a missing value.

OPTION 3   Causes the search for and printing of variable labels to be suppressed.

If you do not select either Option 1 or Option 2, then pairwise deletion of cases is in effect. For tests between groups, a case is ignored in the computation of a *t* if the value for the variable is missing; for tests between variables, a case is ignored if the value for either variable is considered missing.

There are no optional statistics for subprogram T-TEST. Therefore, no STATIS-TICS card is ever used with this procedure.

11.4 EXAMPLE DECK SETUPS FOR SUBPROGRAM T-TEST

Figs. 11.1 and 11.2 have given examples of the printed output from subprogram T-TEST. Example 11.1 shows the deck setup used to generate Fig. 11.1. This is a request for an independent-samples *t*-test where the two groups are whites (category 1) and nonwhites (category 2, where values 3 through 8 have been combined with the original value 2). Option 3 specifies that labels are not to be printed.

```
1               16
RUN NAME        PRINTOUT FOR FIGURE 11.1
GET FILE        ORGSTUDY
RECODE          RACE(3 THRU 8=2)
T-TEST          GROUPS = RACE/ VARIABLES=NMEM,NACT,AGE
OPTIONS         3
FINISH
```

EXAMPLE 11.1

The setup used to generate Fig. 11.2 is very simple. Example 11.2 shows how it was done.

```
1               16
RUN NAME        PRINTOUT FOR FIGURE 11.2
GET FILE        COMSTUDY
T-TEST          PAIRS = POP60 WITH POPLAT
FINISH
```

EXAMPLE 11.2

12
AN OVERVIEW OF THE OTHER FEATURES AVAILABLE IN SPSS

Because this primer is meant only as an introduction to the use of SPSS, we have covered only the basic material necessary for you to begin using this program package. With regard to the data-definition instructions, we have presented the simplest and most commonly used means of describing data to the SPSS program. As you become more familiar with SPSS, you may want to learn about other features which give the system its great versatility. Indeed, you may even find yourself in research situations where some of these other features are required to do the job properly. Similarly, we showed you how to use SPSS only for those statistical procedures which are the basic analytic tools in social statistics. SPSS, of course, has the capability to produce many other types of statistical analyses. With the preparation you have acquired from this primer, you should easily be able to learn how to request these other procedures, as you need them, by reading the SPSS manual.

In this chapter, we will briefly summarize the additional features that are available in the SPSS program. Our purpose here is to inform you of capabilities which you may need at some future time. Because of space limitations, we can only briefly mention the availability of these additional features. Thus, we must depart from our usual practice of carefully defining technical terms and illustrating the use of each capability. The SPSS manual describes all these features in detail, and you are advised to consult that text for further information.

12.1 ADDITIONAL DATA-DEFINITION AND FILE MANAGEMENT FEATURES

As you already know, the regular version of SPSS will handle a maximum of 500 variables. The SPSS miniversion, however, is limited to 100 variables, and the SPSS

100

maxiversion can go up to 1,000 variables at a time. If you have a data set which contains more variables than the limit for the version you wish to use, you may create a special file called an *SPSS archive*. An archive file may store up to 5,000 variables, but the number you may *access* in one run is determined by the version of the program you are using. SPSS also has a feature to add new variables to a file or to delete variables no longer needed.

In Chap. 5, you learned how to use the DATA LIST instruction to name variables and identify their locations on the raw data records. The DATA LIST performs the same functions as the combination of the VARIABLE LIST and INPUT FORMAT cards. You can use the VARIABLE LIST card to name variables and the INPUT FORMAT card to identify their types and locations by means of a Fortran-style format statement. The VARIABLE LIST card and a variation of the INPUT FORMAT card are required when your data are punched in a free-field format or recorded in binary mode. Yet another means of defining variables is with the OSIRIS VARS card. This may be used when you wish to access variables which exist in a system file created by the OSIRIS program, another major statistical package.

A unique feature of SPSS is that your cases may be broken up into *subfiles*. A *subfile* is a contiguous set of cases which you want to handle as a separate unit. In a survey from several different cities, you may want to group the respondents from each city into separate subfiles. Similarly, cases from an experimental group might constitute one subfile, while those from a control group would constitute another subfile. The advantage of subfiles is that you may have the statistical analyses performed separately for each subfile. By using appropriate commands you can also combine subfiles into larger groups or you may have the distinctions between subfiles ignored all together.

Some of the statistical subprograms allow you to supply a matrix of coefficients instead of data cases. For example, the regression and factor analysis subprograms accept a correlation matrix as an alternative input form. They also have the capacity to compute a correlation matrix and send it to an output medium for future use.

12.2 ADDITIONAL RUN CARDS

Several features exist for documenting your printout or system file. A TASK NAME may be printed along with the RUN NAME. The difference between the two is that the TASK NAME may be changed at any point in your program. COMMENT cards may be inserted with your other instructions to serve as printed explanations of what your program instructions are doing. DOCUMENT cards are stored with the system file and can serve as a written description of your data and of changes you may have made to the file. Later, you may ask to have this documentation and other file information listed in your printout or written onto an external medium. Other SPSS run cards allow you to suppress the printing of your SPSS commands or change the maximum number of lines printed per page. You may use the EDIT card to have SPSS check your program for syntax errors and space limitations without actually processing the data and computing statistics.

12.3 ADDITIONAL DATA-MANAGEMENT FEATURES

In Chap. 6, we explained the RECODE card and briefly described the COMPUTE, IF, and COUNT cards. These are very handy commands for changing variables and creating new ones. You may encounter some difficulty with the COMPUTE and IF cards, however, if your data contain missing values. This is so because the computations may be invalid for cases containing missing value codes on the original variables. You may avoid this by using the ASSIGN MISSING card. This instruction causes a missing value code to be assigned to the new variable whenever a missing value code is encountered in any old variable used in that computation.

On occasion, a particular pattern of data transformations needs to be done for quite a few variables. The usual way to handle this is for you to prepare separate transformation cards for each variable involved. This can become very tedious. You may simplify your work, however, by using the DO REPEAT and END REPEAT cards. These instructions define the beginning and ending of a transformation sequence that is to be used repeatedly. They also indicate the variables to be substituted for each execution of the sequence.

SPSS sets aside a certain amount of core storage, called SPACE, for the purpose of storing transformation instructions (TRANSPACE) and for building the tables used in the statistical subprograms (WORKSPACE). The normal amount of SPACE depends upon which version of SPSS you are using and limitations imposed by the local computing facility. You may increase or decrease the total SPACE by adding certain information to the job control statements used to call the SPSS program. Within SPSS itself, you can change the amount of TRANSPACE with the ALLOCATE card. You would want to do this either when you have a large number of data transformations or when you have few transformations but need more WORKSPACE for the statistical calculations.

Other features exist which allow you to ADD CASES to your system file, SORT CASES into a certain order as defined by one or more variables, LIST CASES onto the printer, and WRITE CASES onto an external medium. Numerical weights can be added to the cases for use in the statistical procedures. A random subset of cases may be drawn from your file with the SAMPLE card, or you may use the SELECT IF command to select for processing a subset of cases with specific characteristics. Cases may also be aggregated together to obtain various summary statistics—such as the mean and standard deviation—across all or a subset of cases. These aggregated statistics are then printed and/or written on an external medium.

12.4 ADDITIONAL STATISTICAL SUBPROGRAMS

SPSS contains quite a variety of standard statistical procedures. Periodically new ones are added. The following is a list and brief description of the subprograms available at this writing but not previously described in the primer.

BREAKDOWN   Computes the number of cases, mean, standard deviation, and the sum of scores on a given variable within the categories of one or more control variables. Limited one-way analysis of variance and linearity tests are also available.

NONPAR CORR   Computes Spearman's rho and Kendall's rank order correlation statistics.

PEARSON CORR   Computes Pearson product-moment correlation coefficients with tests for significance.

PARTIAL CORR   Computes partial correlations.

REGRESSION   Computes multiple and stepwise regressions.

FACTOR   Provides principal components and factor analyses with several types of rotations.

CANCORR   Provides a canonical correlation analysis.

ONEWAY   Computes an extensive variety of one-way analyses of variance and tests of significance.

ANOVA   Computes an *n*-way analysis of variance with or without covariates. Multiple classification analysis (MCA) is also available.

DISCRIMINANT   Provides multiple and stepwise discriminant analyses. This subprogram can also compute classifications, plot cases in a one- or two- dimensional discriminant space, and rotate the discriminant space.

GUTTMAN   Provides a Guttman scalogram analysis.

A
DESCRIPTION AND LISTING OF DATA USED IN EXAMPLES

Two sets of data are used throughout the primer to illustrate various points and to provide examples of SPSS printout. This appendix presents a codebook for each study, a listing of the SPSS control cards used to create each system file, and a listing of the actual data cases. Copies of the control cards and data are available to SPSS installations for training and practice purposes. They may be obtained through your local SPSS coordinator.

These data sets, however, are not the complete files from the original studies. No claims are made for the accuracy or validity of the data. Therefore, these data sets are not suitable for research purposes, nor are they meant to be a representative reflection of American life.

In the codebooks, the symbol "(MV)" has been placed after those codes which have been declared as missing values when the SPSS systems files were created.

A.1 AMERICAN SMALL COMMUNITIES STUDY (COMSTUDY)

The American Small Communities Study data file contains aggregate data from 64 small communities in the United States. Each community is a single data case. There are 22 variables measuring population characteristics, magazine subscriptions, and characteristics of the local governmental system. The file name of the SPSS system file created from these data is COMSTUDY.

A1.1 COMSTUDY CODEBOOK

Column(s)	SPSS variable name	Variable description and codes
1–3	COMCODE	Community code number. (Normally, a list of the code numbers and corresponding community names would appear here. This information is not necessary for readers of the primer, so it has been omitted for the sake of brevity.)
5	CARDN01	Card number. (*Note:* Not really necessary, because there is only one card per case. It is included here for the sake of illustration.) 1. First card
7–9	MEDSCH	Median school years for population over 25 years old. (Exact value with *one* decimal digit.) 0. Not ascertained (MV)
11–14	MEDFINC	Median family income. (Exact value.) 0. Not ascertained (MV)
15–18	PTGOHS	Percent of total units of good housing. (Exact value with *one* decimal digit.) 0. Not ascertained (MV)
19–22	PTAGRI	Percent of labor force in agriculture, forestry, and fishing. (Exact value with *one* decimal digit.) 0. Not ascertained (MV)
23–26	PTMANU	Percent of labor force in manual occupations. (Exact value with *one* decimal digit.) 0. Not ascertained (MV)
27–30	PTTERTRY	Percent of labor force in tertiary industries. (Exact value with *one* decimal digit.) 0. Not ascertained (MV)
31–37	POP60	Total community population in 1960. (Exact value.) 0. Not ascertained (MV)
38–44	POPLAT	Total community population at latest estimate. (Exact value.) 0. Not ascertained (MV)
45–49	PTCHNG	Percent population change between 1960 and 1966. (Exact value with *one* decimal digit.) − 100.0 Not ascertained (MV)
50–51	SPISOL	Degree of spatial isolation. 0. No isolation . . . 11. Extreme isolation
52–55	WHTCOLAR	Percent of civilian labor force in white-collar occupations. (Exact value with *one* decimal digit.) 0. Not ascertained (MV)
56–58	LIFE	*Life Magazine* sales per 1,000 population. (Exact value.) 0. Not ascertained (MV)

A1.1 COMSTUDY CODEBOOK *(continued)*

Column(s)	SPSS variable name	Variable description and codes
59–61	TIME	*Time Magazine* sales per 1,000 population. (Exact value.) 0. Not ascertained (MV)
62–64	NEWSWEEK	*Newsweek* sales per 1,000 population. (Exact value.) 0. Not ascertained (MV)
65–67	READDIG	*Reader's Digest* sales per 1,000 population. (Exact value.) 0. Not ascertained (MV)
68	HRSWORK	Number of hours per week worked by head of government. 1. Less than 5 hours 2. 6–10 hours 3. 11–20 hours 4. 21–30 hours 5. 31–40 hours 6. Over 40 hours 8. Inapplicable (MV) 9. Not ascertained (MV)
69	GOVSELCT	Method of selecting head of government. 1. Direct election 2. Elected by local board 3. Appointed by a higher authority 4. Other 8. No local head of government (MV) 9. Not ascertained (MV)
70	CONELECT	Whether elections for head of government are contested. 1. Always contested 2. Usually contested 3. Occasionally contested 4. Never contested 8. Appointed or no head of government (MV) 9. Not ascertained (MV)
71	PARTISAN	Whether election of head of government is legally partisan. 1. Nonpartisan by law 2. Partisan 8. Appointed or no head of government (MV) 9. Not ascertained (MV)
72	PARTROLE	Actual role of parties in the election of head of government. 1. Candidates run with party label 2. Candidates run with no label but with party affiliation 3. Totally nonpartisan 8. Appointed or no head of government (MV) 9. Not ascertained (MV)

A.1.2 DATA-DEFINITION CARDS FOR COMSTUDY FILE

```
1                  16
FILE NAME          COMSTUDY, STUDY OF AMERICAN SMALL COMMUNITIES
DATA LIST          FIXED(1)/1 COMCODE 1-3, CARDNO1 5, MEDSCH 7-9 (1), MEDFINC 11-14,
                   PTGOHS PTAGRI PTMANU PTTERTRY 15-30 (1), POP60 POPLAT 31-44,
                   PTCHNG 45-49 (1), SPISOL 50-51, WHTCOLAR 52-55 (1), LIFE TIME
                   NEWSWEEK READDIG 56-67, HRSWORK GOVSELCT CONELECT PARTISAN
                   PARTROLE 68-72
INPUT MEDIUM       CARD
N OF CASES         64
VAR LABELS         COMCODE COMMUNITY CODE/
                   CARDNO1 CARD NUMBER/
                   MEDSCH MEDIAN SCHOOL YRS FOR POPULATION OVER 25/
                   MEDFINC MEDIAN FAMILY INCOME/
                   PTGOHS PERCENT TOTAL UNITS GOOD HOUSING/
                   PTAGRI PERCENT LABOR IN AGRICULTURE-FOREST-FISH/
                   PTMANU, PERCENT LABOR IN MANUAL OCCUPATIONS/
                   PTTERTRY,PERCENT LABOR IN TERTIARY INDUSTRY/
                   POP60,TOTAL POPULATION IN 1960/
                   POPLAT, TOTAL POPULATION LATEST ESTIMATE/
                   PTCHNG,PERCENT POPULATION CHANGE 1960-66/
                   SPISOL,DEGREE OF SPATIAL ISOLATION/
                   WHTCOLAR,PERCENT LABOR IN WHITE COLLAR JOBS/
                   LIFE,LIFE MAGAZINE SALES PER 1000 POPULATION/
                   TIME,TIME MAGAZINE SALES PER 1000 POPULATION/
                   NEWSWEEK,NEWSWEEK SALES PER 1000 POPULATION/
                   READDIG,READERS DIGEST SALES PER 1000 POPULATION/
                   HRSWORK,WORKING HOURS PER WEEK HEAD OF GOVT/
                   GOVSELCT,METHOD OF SELECTING HEAD OF GOVERNMENT/
                   CONELECT,ELECTION OF HEAD OF GOVERNMENT CONTESTED/
                   PARTISAN,ELECTION HEAD LEGALLY PARTISAN/
                   PARTROLE,ACTUAL ROLE OF PARTIES IN ELECTING HEAD
VALUE LABELS       HRSWORK (1)LESS THAN 5 HRS (2)6-10 HRS (3)11-20 HRS
                   (4)21-30 HRS (5)31-40 HRS (6)OVER 40 HRS
                   (8)INAPPLICABLE (9)NA/
                   GOVSELCT (1)DIRECT ELECTION (2)ELECT LOCAL BOARD
                   (3)APPOINTED BY HIGHER ATH (4)OTHER (8)NO LOCAL HEAD
                   (9)NA/
                   CONELECT (1)ALWAYS CONTESTED (2)USUALLY CONTESTED
                   (3)OCCASIONALLY CONTEST (4)NEVER CONTESTED
                   (8)APPOINTED OR NONE(9)NA/
                   PARTISAN (1)NONPARTISAN BY LAW (2)PARTISAN (8)APPOINTED OR NONE
                   (9)NA/
                   PARTROLE (1)RUN WITH PARTY LABEL (2) NO LABEL BUT AFFIL
                   (3)TOTALLY NONPARTISON (8)APPOINTED OR NONE(9)NA
MISSING VALUES     HRSWORK TO PARTROLE (8,9)/PTCHNG(-100)/
                   MEDSCH TO POPLAT, WHTCOLAR TO READDIG(0)
```

A.1.3 DATA CASES FOR COMSTUDY FILE

```
 22 1  86 5097 217 720  33 247   8350       0-1000  4 170   0   0   0  041321
 41 1  86 2757 557 613 151 168    417       0-100010 168   0   0   0  043888
 61 1  95 6100 819   5 426 355  19062  21200  112 0 339 39   7   5 8541222
 72 1  94 4917 775 262  61 471  11913  13400  125 5 408 34  10   8 7641313
 81 1 126 8191 946  17 213 574  40568  42800   55 0 622 68  34  12  041122
 82 1 114 6718 977  17 294 350  24723  30000  213 0 327102  25 2231231221
123 1  85 4417 568 102 150 451   4835   6000  241 8 259   0   0   0 6741321
131 1 121 7908 873  85 574 341   4785   5300  108 5 628 91  50  22 9941122
141 1 119 4444 966  16  66 569   3197  11000 2441 9 555 34  15   0  099999
142 1 101 3685 723   6  32 517   3157   3157    0 9 334 84  36 6377288888
152 1  94 5278   0  16 176 424  20117       0-1000  1 352   0   0   0  043888
181 1  98 5963 778 341 325 334  11880       0-1000  6 400   0   4   4 6841221
231 1 108 4655   0 358 223 262    538       0-100010  13   0   0   0  043888
232 1 121 5815 701  12 278 526   2517   2517   010 498 91  21 2326341113
241 1 108 6632 601 310 341 349  17184       0-100010 403   0   0   0  041213
261 1  99 6340 501 295 475 243   1217       0-1000  2 280   0   0   0  041321
272 1 114 4513 623 165   7 517   1674       0-100010 421   0  17  017941113
281 1 120 4786 698  36 181 533   3028   3028   010 440 32  12 1014542888
291 1  74 1678 790 338  56 327   3986       0-100010 211   0   0   0  044888
292 1 108 4439 806   9  59 536   7819       0-100010 541 27   7   7 9551113
301 1  89 4189 568  21 347 375  15193  15500   20 7 368 13   4   5 6021213
311 1  65 2894 647  75  79 441   6468   6468    0 9 322 25   8   0 2952888
321 1 119 4050 703  42 268 379   1715   1750   2010 376 79  31 1820751121
342 1  89 3980 409 142 419 295   1160       0-100010 301   0   0 1320051213
352 1  94 6405 621 366  94 538   1196       0-100010 363347  81 4659651313
391 1  88 3242   0  83 330 275    541       0-100010 239   0   0   0  054888
412 1  86 6375 855 201 443 354  49658       0-1000  3 298 30   7   4 7851213
421 1 137 7171 915   6 367 399  15173  24789  634 7 446   0   4   0  051322
442 1 119 5595 762   4  47 466  17731  16800  -53 8 487 46  27 1212652888
451 1 117 7216 952   4 408 373  18676  20300   87 7 469 19   6   0  051222
471 1 122 6279 765  31  45 550  10740  11800   99 8 463 46  22 2214151313
482 1  95 4092 844 115  67 560   1513       0-100011 409   0 4328819452888
491 1  86 6291 906   2 585 260  29253  29300    2 6 281 64   6   4 5731222
502 1 102 5956 755  10 300 421  35789  33500  -64 3 428 53  18  32 8151313
513 1  93 5862 689   0 435 302   5862       0-1000  7 262   0   0   0  051113
542 1 128 8517 948 348 126 526  11037       0-1000  3 510   0   0   0  021213
552 1 121 7244 822   1 345 476  21261  21146   -5 4 578104  61   0  051313
581 1 118 8463 941   2 248 541  17499  17762   15 3 640121  40 3823551113
622 1  86 4827 659   5 469 311  37276  45429  219 6 319 36   8   7 9152888
632 1 102 4410 729  15 301 455   6159   6159    0 7 406 55  22 1725152888
651 1 122 5849 781  11  71 624  34451  38500  11811 530 56  43 2311451113
661 1 101 4703 524  90  41 622   1566       0-100011 590   0  20  017564888
672 1  94 6879 968 230 540 229   9286       0-1000  2 322   0  16  11 5661322
682 1 125 9384 995   5 382 468  16805  18500  101 3 658 75  32   0  061113
692 1 105 5155 756  25 385 415   3116   3116    0 8 357 42  33 1117761222
711 1 121 6000 881  14 385 644  24411  25500   45 7 525 36  17 1514262888
721 1  87 2942   0 463  74 379    239       0-100011 368   0   0   0  061121
732 1 110 5945 680  35 210 498   3263   3594  101 9 420 53  33 2020261221
742 1 113 6005   0 151 179 465   3084       0-1000  6 383   0   0   0  061421
743 1 115 5859 831  19 121 645  49142  63500  292 6 552 71  35 1917361121
751 1 122 7475 908 327 288 385  25952  32283  244 1 562   0   0   0  061213
781 1  90 4338 741   0 436 384   5958   5958    0 9 357 21   8  14 7021413
782 1  72 5339   0  91 212 394    661       0-1000  9 205   0   0   0  061121
791 1 114 6828 928   5 423 372   7249   8800  214 6 448 95  22 1113488888
802 1  90 4406 845   6 306 424  13674  12600  -79 8 373 62  14  813731422
821 1 109 5313 780  11 385 368   3982   3982    0 7 410 35  14 2012161113
831 1  63 2326 316  73 352 258    700       0-1000  9 258   0   0   0  061213
861 1 104 4745 665  70 301 395   4642   4642    0 5 426 27  11   0 8261413
881 1 125 5142 843  31  21 266   5864   8500  450 7 469 42  29 2211161113
891 1 121 5478 772  15 177 478  51230  56000  9310 502 34  13  810061213
893 1  89 3327 582 485 201 314   3335       0-100010 385   0   0   0  061421
912 1 113 5521 849  11 197 511   9520  10300   82 4 395   0   0   0  061113
932 1   0    0   0   0   0   0  49845       0-1000  3   0   0   0   0  061221
951 1 118 6390 788   9 277 515  37987  38600   16 6 489 65  30  15  061422
```

A.2 ORGANIZATIONAL MEMBERSHIP AND ACTIVITY STUDY (ORGSTUDY)

The Organizational Membership and Activity Study data file contains survey responses from 350 individual persons. Each individual is a single data case. There are 29 variables measuring the individual's demographic characteristics and membership in a variety of organizations. The file name of the SPSS system file created from these data is ORGSTUDY.

A.2.1 ORGSTUDY CODEBOOK

Column(s)	SPSS variable name	Variable description and codes
1–3	COMMID	Identification number of the community in which the respondent lives. (Normally, a list of the code numbers and corresponding names would appear here. This information is not necessary for readers of the primer, so it has been omitted for the sake of brevity.)
4–5	RESPID	Respondent's identification number within the community.
7	RESDYTH	Type of residence where respondent lived during first 15 years of his/her life. 1. Mostly farm 2. Mostly small town 3. Mostly small city 4. Mostly big city 9. Not ascertained; does not know (MV) 0. Inapplicable (MV)
8	MARITAL	Marital status. 1. Married 2. Widowed 3. Divorced 4. Separated 5. Never married
		Note: The following membership questions have the same coding categories, which are as follows: 0. No 1. Yes 8. Not ascertained (MV)
9	FRATMEM	Has membership in a fraternal organization.
10	SERVMEM	Has membership in a service club.
11	VETMEM	Has membership in a veterans group.
12	POLMEM	Has membership in a political organization.
13	UNIONMEM	Has membership in a labor union.
14	SPORTMEM	Has membership in a sports club.
15	YOUTHMEM	Has membership in a youth group.
16	SCHOLMEM	Has membership in a school service group.
17	HOBMEM	Has membership in a hobby or garden club.
18	SCHFRMEM	Has membership in a school fraternity or sorority.
19	NATMEM	Has membership in a national organization.
20	FARMEM	Has membership in a farm organization.
21	LITMEM	Has membership in a literary or arts group.
22	PROFMEM	Has membership in a professional or academic organization.
23	RELMEM	Has membership in a religious organization.
24	OTHMEM	Has other memberships.

A.2.1 ORGSTUDY CODEBOOK (continued)

Column(s)	SPSS variable name	Variable description and codes
25	NMEM	Total number of memberships. (Exact value, with the highest being 7.)
26	NACT	Number of active memberships. (Exact value, with the highest being 7.)
27	RELIG	Religious affiliation. 1. Protestant 2. Catholic 3. Jewish 4. Shinto or Tao 5. None 6. Orthodox Catholic 7. Buddhist or Confucian 8. Hindu or Muslim 9. Other non-Protestant group 0. Not ascertained (MV)
28–29	AGE	Age at last birthday. (Exact value.) 18. . . . 87. 98. Does not know or refused (MV) 99. Not ascertained (MV)
30–31	INCOME	Family income. 1. Less than $1,000 2. $1,000–$1,999 3. $2,000–$2,999 4. $3,000–$3,999 5. $4,000–$4,999 6. $5,000–$5,999 7. $6,000–$6,999 11. $7,000–$7,999 21. $8,000–$8,999 31. $9,000–$9,999 41. $10,000–$14,999 51. $15,000–$19,999 61. $20,000–$24,999 71. $25,000 and over 88. Refused (MV) 99. Do not know (MV)
33	EDRESPON	Last year of school completed by respondent. 1. None 2. 1–8 years 3. 9–11 years 4. 12 years 5. Some college but not completed 6. College graduate 7. Schooling beyond college 9. Do not know (MV) 0. Not ascertained (MV)
34	SEX	Sex of respondent. 1. Male 2. Female
35	RACE	Race of respondent. 1. White 2. Negro 3. Oriental 4. American Indian 5. Latin American 8. Other 0. Not ascertained (MV)

A.2.1 ORGSTUDY CODEBOOK (continued)

Column(s)	SPSS variable name	Variable description and codes
36	OCLEVRES	Occupational level of the respondent.
		1. Unskilled
		2. Ambiguous skill
		3. Independent craftsman
		4. Skilled
		5. Clerical, sales, and lower-level technical
		6. Professional and managerial
		0. Other

A.2.2 DATA-DEFINITION CARDS FOR ORGSTUDY FILE

```
1                       16
FILE NAME               ORGSTUDY,STUDY OF ORGANIZATIONAL MEMBERSHIP AND ACTIVITY
DATA LIST               FIXED/ 1 COMMID 1-3, RESPID 4-5, RESDYTH MARITAL FRATMEM SERVMEM
                        VETMEM POLMEM UNIONMEM SPORTMEM YOUTHMEM SCHOLMEM HOBMEM
                        SCHFRMEM NATMEM FARMEM LITMEM PROFMEM RELMEM OTHMEM NMEM NACT
                        RELIG 7-27, AGE INCOME 28-31, EDRESPON SEX RACE OCLEVRES 33-36
INPUT MEDIUM            CARD
N OF CASES             350
VAR LABELS              COMMID,COMMUNITY ID NUMBER/
                        RESPID,RESPONDENT ID NUMBER/
                        RESDYTH,RESIDENCE DURING FIRST 15 YEARS/
                        MARITAL,MARITAL STATUS/
                        FRATMEM,MEMBER IN FRATERNAL ORGANIZATION/
                        SERVMEM,MEMBER IN SERVICE CLUB/
                        VETMEM,MEMBER IN VETERANS GROUP/
                        POLMEM,MEMBER IN POLITICAL ORGANIZATION/
                        UNIONMEM,MEMBER IN LABOR UNION/
                        SPORTMEM,MEMBER IN SPORTS CLUB/
                        YOUTHMEM,MEMBER IN YOUTH GROUP/
                        SCHOLMEM,MEMBER IN SCHOOL SERVICE GROUP/
                        HOBMEM,MEMBER IN HOBBY-GARDEN CLUB/
                        SCHFRMEM,MEMBER IN SCHOOL FRATERNITY-SORORITY/
                        NATMEM,MEMBER IN ANY NATIONAL ORGANIZATION/
                        FARMEM,MEMBER IN FARM ORGANIZATION/
                        LITMEM,MEMBER IN LIT-ART GROUPS/
                        PROFMEM,MEMBER IN PROF-ACADEMIC ORGANIZATION/
                        RELMEM,MEMBER IN RELIGIOUS ORGANIZATION/
                        OTHMEM,OTHER MEMBERSHIPS/
                        NMEM,TOTAL NUMBER OF MEMBERSHIPS/
                        NACT,TOTAL NUMBER ACTIVE MEMBERSHIPS/
                        RELIG,RELIGIOUS AFFILIATION/
                        AGE,AGE AT LAST BIRTHDAY/
                        INCOME,FAMILY INCOME/
                        EDRESPON,LAST YEAR OF SCHOOL COMPLETED/
                        SEX,RESPONDENT'S SEX/
                        RACE,RESPONDENT'S RACE/
                        OCLEVRES,OCCUPATIONAL LEVEL OF RESPONDENT
VALUE LABELS            RESDYTH (1)MOSTLY FARM(2)MSTLY SMALL TOWN (3)MSTLY SMALL CITY
                            (4)MSTLY BIG CITY,SUBN(9)NA,DK(0)INAPPLICABLE/
                        MARITAL (1)MARRIED(2)WIDOWED(3)DIVORCED(4)SEPARATED
                            (5)NEVER MARRIED/
                        FRATMEM TO OTHMEM (1)YES(0)NO(8)NA/
                        NMEM,NACT(0)NONE(1)ONE(2)TWO(3)THREE(4)FOUR(5)FIVE(6)SIX(7)SEVEN/
                        RELIG (1)PROTESTANT(2)CATHOLIC(3)JEWISH(4)SHINTO,TAO(5)NONE
                            (6)ORTHODOX(7)BUDDHIST,CONF(8)HINDU,MUSLIM
                            (9)OTHER NON-PROTESTANT(0)NA/
                        INCOME (1)LESS THAN 1000(2)1000-1999(3)2000-2999(4)3000-3999
                            (5)4000-4999(6)5000-5999(7)6000-6999(11)7000-7999
                            (21)8000-8999(31)9000-9999(41)10000-14999(51)15000-19999
                            (61)20000-24999(71)25000 AND OVER(88)REFUSED(99)DK/
                        EDRESPON (1)NONE(2)1-8 YEARS (3)9-11 YEARS(4)12 YEARS
                                (5)COLLEGE INCOMPLETE(6)COLLEGE GRADUATE(7)COLLEGE PLUS
                                (9)DK(0)NA/
                        SEX (1)MALE(2)FEMALE/
                        RACE (1)WHITE(2)NEGRO(3)ORIENTAL(4)AMERICAN INDIAN
                            (5)LATIN AMERICAN(8)OTHER(0)NA/
                        OCLEVRES (1)UNSKILLED(2)AMBIGUOUS SKILL (3)INDEPENDENTS(4)SKILLED
                            (5)CLRC,SALES,LOW TECH(6)PROFESSIONAL,MANG(0)OTHER
MISSING VALUES          RESDYTH(0,9)/ FRATMEM TO OTHMEM(8)/
                        AGE(98,99)/INCOME(88,99)/EDRESPON(0,9)/
                        RELIG,RACE(0)/
```

```
11 1 42000000000000000000176 3 2215        4122 21000000000000000000130 1 3212
11 2 11000000000000000000124 6 3210          42 1 21000000000000000000127 6 4210
11 3 11000000000000000000150 4 2114          42 2 11000000000000000000138 4 3210
11 4 11000000000000000000124 7 2112          42 3 11000000000000000000153 1 2210
11 5 11000000000000000000014141 4212          42 4 11000101000000000011133 7 3215
11 6 01000000000000000000140 7 4115          42 5 11000000000000000000172 1 2113
11 7 11000000000000000000013421 4215          42 6 11100100000000000011164 4 2113
11 8 31100000000000000001115441 5116          42 7 11000000000000000000141 5 5112
11 9 31000000000000000000145 2 2220          43 1 11000000000000000015241 3116
1110 05000000000000000000125 1 3122          43 2 01000000011000000002124211 4215
1111 95000000000000000000129 2 3221          43 3 21000000000000000012421 4210
1112 01000000000000000000126 1 3221          43 4 02000000000000000000169 2 2210
1113 01000000000000000000126 2 3221          43 5 11100000000000000011163 3 2122
1114 92000000000000000110165 1 4121          43 6 11000000000000000000152 2 2210
1115 01000000000000000000137 3 2122          43 7 21000000000000000000125 4 4111
21 1 42000000000000001011179 6 3210          51 1 41000100000000000000181 7 4116
21 2 11000000000000000015711 3210          51 2 32000000000000000000179 3 4212
21 3 22000000000000001012115488 4215          51 3 41000000001000000010559 7 5113
21 4 21100010010000000003116711 5112          51 4 41000000000000000000525 6 6215
21 5 21000000000000001001015488 3116          51 5 45000000000000000000324 1 5110
21 6 21000010000000000001014888 4114          51 6 42000000001000000121383 5 3210
21 7 12000000001000000000011149 6 4215          51 7 41000000000000000100010524 5 6215
21 8 12000000000000000000138 1 2221          61 1 11000010000000000010275 4 3112
21 9 14000000000000000000151 1 2222          61 2 03000010000000000121228 6 5115
2110 13000010000000000010154 4 2121          61 3 11000010000000000001015621 4112
2111 12000010000000000010173 2 2121          61 4 01110000100000000003224841 2114
2112 01000010000000000000129 4 4124          61 5 02010010000000000021260 6 2211
2113 13000000000000000000174 3 2122          61 6 21100000000000000010178 4 1210
2114 45000000000000000000144 1 4221          61 7 41000000000010000011253 7 7230
2115 45000000000000000000135 3 4221          61 8 41000010000000000102024621 2210
22 1 01000010000000001021123 4 4122          61 9 24000000000000000000142 4 2221
22 2 15000000000000000000125 4 3222          6110 01100000010000000022141 3 3220
22 3 21000010000000000001114441 2122          6111 35000000000000000000126 2 3221
22 4 11000100000000000000164 2 2122          6112 05000000000000010122253 5 4116
22 5 11000000000000000110161 5 2220          6113 22000000000000000000266 2 2112
22 6 11100000010000000002113311 3220          6114 25000000000000000000228 6 2112
22 7 12100000000000000010166 3 2220          6115 21000000000000000000265 6 1112
22 8 11000010000000000010154 4 2124          6116 21000000000000000001011139 3 3222
22 9 14000000000000000110140 2 2221          6117 14000010000000000001113371 2121
2210 11100000000000000120165 4 2220          6118 45000010000010000021253 5 4111
2211 21000000000000000110129 3 2220          6119 21000000010000000011127 4 4210
2212 41000010000000000011152 4 3124          6120 41000010000000000001014311 2112
2213 21000000000000000000141 6 2220          6121 01001100010000000021125 7 3210
2214 41000000000000000000121 4 4121          6122 21000000000000000000246 7 3210
2215 11000000000000000000168 3 2220          6123 01000000000000000000218 2 3211
2216 25000000000000000000124 4 4221          71 1 41000000010000000011113831 4210
2217 21000000010000000011163 5 4221          71 2 41000010000000000011548 7 3112
2218 41000000000000000000013511 4222          71 3 01100000000000000001012841 4210
2219 15000000000000000000149 7 3221          71 4 11000000011000000002223041 4210
2220 21000000000000000000137 5 4124          71 5 41000011000000000002215131 3115
2221 41100101110110010007713951 6120          71 6 11000010000000000010014731 4115
2222 31000000010000000000011173 3 6220          71 7 21100010000000000002115071 4114
31 1 01000000000000000000246 7 1210          71 8 31010000000000001002213951 3115
31 2 11000000000000000000126 7 4115          72 1 31010000000000000001156011 2113
31 3 41000000000000000000013611 6113          72 2 11100010000000000013057388 2116
31 4 21011011000000000004104388 6115          72 3 11000000000000000000258 6 5114
31 5 11010000000000000000011160 4 5216          72 4 12101000000000000011441744 1 5216
31 6 11000000000000001001114411 5115          72 5 11001000000000000001027611 2113
31 7 01000000000000000000548 7 2210          72 6 11000000000000000001010177 3 2210
31 8 21000000000000000000120 3 2210          72 7 11000000001000000102214841 3212
31 9 22000000000000000000164 3 3212          72 8 21000000000000000000162 1 2220
3110 11000000000000000000128 7 3210          72 9 21000000000000000014121 3210
3111 21100010000000000002215911 2114          7210 21000000000000000014511 4221
3112 31000010000000000011235 3 4114          7211 31000000000000000000158 2 1111
3113 11000000000000000000175 5 5116          7212 11000000000000000015511 2123
3114 21000000000000000000157 5 3113          7213 21000000000000000000160 3 2121
3115 11000000000000001011174 2 2210          7214 11000000000000000000243 4 2111
41 1 11000000000000000000156 4 2210          7215 12000000000000000000187 1 2210
41 2 01000000010000000011127 6 3210          7216 21000000000000000015811 6216
41 3 11000000000000000000156 3 2210          7217 22000000000000000018499 2210
41 4 11000000000000000000167 3 2112          7218 25001010000010000030269 1 2111
41 5 11000000000000000000122 5 4214          7219 11100000000000000001015711 3113
41 6 11000000000000000000153 3 2112          7220 21000000000000000000262 3 2111
41 7 11000000000000000000170 3 2113          7221 21000000000100000001016541 6135
41 8 11001000000001000022141 4 4111          7222 14000000000000000000142 2 2211
41 9 11000000000000000000146 1 2113          81 1 41000000000000000111126 6 4210
4110 11000000000000000000168 1 2210          81 2 11000000000000000000172 5 2112
4111 01000000000000000000159 6 2113          81 3 31000011000100000033142 4 6122
4112 11000000000000000000137 2 2210          81 4 41000000000000000000225 6 3154
4113 11000000000000000000172 2 2210          81 5 11000000000000000000257 5 3215
4114 11000000001000000001114099 3212          81 6 41000000001000000011124051 4215
4115 11000000010000000011248 4 4210          81 7 21000000000000000000220 7 3210
4116 11000000000000000000152 1 2111          81 8 21010000010000000022115461 5210
4117 21000000100010000002112551 5210          81 9 22011000000000000022116711 6116
4118 21000000010000000010014899 2210          8110 31010000011000000033315071 7210
4119 11000000000000000000550 1 1111          8111 23000000000000000000124 4 4111
4120 41000000010001000022113451 5210          8112 21000000000000000000033051 7215
4121 11001000000000000010176 2 2113          8113 21010000110000001004113541 6116
```

(continued)

```
8114 12000000000000000000000558 5 4214        112 1 11000010000000000010148 2 2122
8115 31000000000000000000013551   4210        112 2 21000000000000000000142 5 4220
8116 41000000000000000000014151   4215        112 3 11000000000000000000146 7 3124
8117 21080100110000000002215061 4210          112 4 41000000010000000001124621 2210
8118 41000001000000000012112221 3113          112 5 45000000000000000000000247 2 2112
8119 12000000000000000000155 6 4215           112 6 11000000000000000000229 2 4210
8120 11000010000000000001115921 2112          112 7 11000010000000000001022621 3114
8121 31100010000000000002125841 4112          113 1 21000000000000000000011911 3210
8122 42000001810000011004214621 7216          113 2 21000010000000000012014431 4212
82 1 14000000000000000000111159 6 5111        113 3 21100000000000000113315521 2212
82 2 41000000000000000011022431 4210          113 4 31000001000000000001123331 5112
82 3 41000010010000000021136 7 4215           113 5 01010010000000000002012231 4112
82 4 11000011110000000004214711 5210          113 6 23000000000000000000025831 4112
82 5 21000010000000000001122411 4114          113 7 11000000010000000102273721 4230
82 6 21000000000000000000013041 4112          121 1 41000000000000000000126 6 4210
82 7 21000010010000000002024231 3112          121 2 21000000000000000000015621 2210
82 8 41000000000000000000022921 3250          121 3 21000000110000000002145 7 5210
82 9 41000000000000000000012321 5210          121 4 13000010000000000011564 4 2112
8210 45000000000000000000012441 5110          121 5 91000010100000000021126 3 5110
8211 21100000000000000010149 6 4115           121 6 21000010000000000010014741 2111
8212 41000010000000000001023121 4154          121 7 21000000000000000000054711 2212
8213 11000000000000000000142 4 4114           122 1 31000010000000000001012041 4215
8214 41000000000000000000013011 4215          122 2 41000000000000000010024511 4250
8216 25010001010000100041218 7 4215           122 3 21100000000000000011218 6 4210
8217 11101001000000000003013151 5114          122 4 25000001100000000002112131 5215
8218 41000011001001000003222421 3114          122 5 45000000000000000000121 2 5110
8219 21000000000000000000022011 3210          122 6 41111010110000000017414051 5115
8220 41000000000000000000013121 3212          122 7 11001000001000000021570 4 2113
8221 41000010000000000012123341 5116          122 8 31000000000000000000014411 2114
8222 31000010000000000001123041 4114          123 1 11000010000000000010154 3 2112
83 1 41000000010000000001113821 4230          123 2 21000000000000000000146 4 3210
83 2 21000100000000000000016241 6210          123 3 21000010000000000001012731 4112
83 3 21000000100000100020141S1 7116          123 4 21000000000000000000127 6 3210
83 4 41011001100000001052132A1 6116          123 5 21000000000000000000118 5 3210
83 5 31000001000000100211565I 5116            123 6 11000000000000000000183 2 1112
83 6 13000000000000100111571I 4213            123 7 11000010000000000010275 3 2114
83 7 01000100000000000013441 4115             123 8 41000000000000000000523 1 3211
83 8 31000000000000000000094721 4210          123 9 22000000000000000000017499 3216
83 9 11010010000000000211644I 6115            12310 14000010000000000011157 6 2114
8310 21000000000000000000026841 5115          12311 21000011000000000002213011 3112
8311 42010000000000000001037311 3210          12312 11000000010000000010525 6 3210
8312 21001100000000000012114841 4115          12313 11000000110000000022155 5 3210
8313 23010000000010110044345 7 6215           12314 41000000000000000100010127 7 4215
8314 41100000000000000012197441 5116          12315 11001000000000000010131II 5110
8315 01000000000000000000223 7 5215           12316 41000010000000000010124 6 4110
8316 11000000010000000011142 6 2220           12317 01000010000000000010126 7 5210
8317 44000000000010000010121 5 5220           12318 31000010010000000020125311 5210
8318 22000000000000000000174 3 2121            12319 11000000000000000000237 6 2210
8319 01000000000000000000023131 3112          12320 41000010100000000021131 7 5110
8320 12000010000010000022156 6 3222           12321 21100001111000000005414131 7120
8321 41000000000000000000123 6 4124            12322 24000000000000000000012241 4114
8322 01000001000001000022122 5 5225           12323 31000000080000000000053551 5116
84 1 41000000011100000030136441 6210          131 1 12000000000000000000017399 2210
84 2 21100010001000000002015271 7216          131 2 41000000000000000000022741 6116
84 3 01000001010000000002013511 5215          131 3 41000000000000000000137 7 5210
84 4 41000000000000000000024751 6115           131 4 41000100000000100I024151 4215
84 5 41110100000000000002215351 6116          131 5 41000101110000000003313971 5210
84 6 41000010000000000001055921 4114           131 6 21100000000000I000021140 7 3113
84 7 41000000000000000017141 4114              131 7 21000001000000000011133441 4112
91 1 41000000000000000000129 7 4210            131 8 21000000000000000014421 3210
91 2 11000000000000000000136 7 4215            131 9 21000010000000000010122 7 4212
91 3 21000000000000000000052331 4212           13110 21000000000000000017421 2114
91 4 21001000000000000011147411 5210           13111 21000000000000112123021 6210
91 5 41000000000000000000175 2 2114             13112 21000010000000000011221 3 4112
91 6 11000010001000000131171 4 2112            13113 41000000000000001011267 3 2210
91 7 31000010000000000001062141 4114           13114 41001010000000000020274 4 2112
91 8 14000000000000000000174 2 2222            13115 33000000000000000000248 6 3112
91 9 21000000000000000000235 6 5152            13116 31000000000000000000024741 3215
9110 93000000000000000000244 3 4250            13117 41000000000000000111170 2 2114
9111 21000000000000000000231 7 2210            13118 21000000000000000015341 4210
9112 31000000000000000000262 4 2152            13119 41000100000000000025541 2214
9113 24000000000000010011139 1 4225            13120 21000000000000000111158 7 4114
9114 41000100000000000000526 7 4121            13121 31000010000000000011123 7 4114
101 1 22000000000100010020158 6 7216           13122 32000000000000000000247 3 2212
101 2 01101000000000010003336461 7116          132 1 31001010100000000003324041 3112
101 3 41000000101001100422305I 7116            132 2 01000000000000000000022141 2212
101 4 41100000010100110050139411 7210          132 3 25001001000001100422254I 5114
101 5 01000000000000000014171 5210              132 4 31000100100000000002224041 4215
101 6 43001001001000010040261611 6115          132 5 91000000000000000000274 3 1112
101 7 35000001010100110050125211 5215          132 6 41000110000010000021230 6 2112
111 1 11010000000000000001112651 5214          132 7 01000000000000000000023221 3210
111 2 31001000000000000010246411 4112          132 8 22000000000000000000269 4 2210
111 3 41000000010000100021133441 6210          132 9 31000000111001000040227411 6210
111 4 21000000010000000001112641 4210          13210 05000000000000000000022521 4115
111 5 41000100100000000022143311 3215          13211 01000110010000000020236 7 3114
111 6 45000000100000100221131411 6116          13212 05000000001000000010231511 5115
111 7 41000000000000000000055841 3116
```

B
SPSS CONTENTS

12

CREATING, RETRIEVING, AND MANIPULATING FILES WITH MORE THAN 500 VARIABLES: GET ARCHIVE, SAVE ARCHIVE, AND LIST ARCHINFO CARDS

13

EDITING SPSS CONTROL-CARD DECKS: THE EDIT FACILITY

APPENDIXES

INDEX